✳ The New York Book of Shops

2nd edition

By Ranjani
Gopalarathinam

universe publishing

First published in the United States of America in 2005
by Universe Publishing
a division of Rizzoli International Publications, Inc.
300 Park Avenue South
New York, New York 10010
www.rizzoliusa.com

© 2008, 2004 by Ranjani Gopalarathinam
Design by Paul Kepple and Susan Van Horn at Headcase Design
www.headcasedesign.com
Cover illustration by Sujean Rim
Typeset by Tina Henderson

2005 2006 2007 2008 2009 / 10 9 8 7 6 5 4 3 2 1
Distributed to the U.S. trade by Random House, New York
Printed in the United States of America
ISBN: 978-0-7893-1688-2
Library of Congress Catalog Control Number: 2007910366

Publisher's Note
Neither Universe nor the author has any interest, financial or personal, in
the establishments listed in this book. No fees were paid or services
rendered in exchange for inclusion in these pages. While every effort was
made to ensure accuracy at the time of publication, it is always best to call
ahead and confirm that the information is up-to-date.

contents

Introduction

Shopping in New York City is not just a pastime; it is a way of life. For native New Yorkers, knowing the best places to shop for virtually anything (in a city where every imaginable thing is available) is a form of urban prowess, ducking and diving through the city blocks like stealthy superheroes to find the best of what the city has to offer. For visitors, the city is rife with people and activity the likes of which are unparalleled anywhere else, so even the smallest bit of information can be the chisel you need to start chipping away New York's intimidating exterior. Whichever category you fall into, there is much to explore, and the city's mystery is part of what makes the hunt so tantalizing.

If you love to shop, New York City will be the apex of your shopping life. If you are more interested in the cultural fabric of the city, shopping will give you an excuse, if not a great lens, on the kaleidoscope of neighborhoods, people, and hidden secrets that New York City offers. Whatever your motivation, the city is always one step ahead of you. With this guide, you can keep up with the brisk step of New Yorkers while taking a tour of the city via its one-of-a-kind shops.

I have included veteran little shops, some exciting new spaces to check out in 2008, as well as numerous neighborhood R&R stops any shopping day-tripper would enjoy. (Look to the sidebars for things to do while wandering through different neighborhoods.) Many of these shops are worth the visit whether you are buying or browsing, because part of the fun is in the journey. Other shops have a museum-like reverence for their wares (be it buttons or bathing suits) run by owners who carefully curate their selection of items so that you are seeing only the best and most representative items from upcoming lines, a service that spares you the hassle of wading through each season's fresh crop of new designers.

The city is a puzzle of these little niches and viewpoints, and why New York City shopping is world famous.

While doing research for this book, I met some wonderful individuals in the different retail communities of the city, and I hope you will find the people you meet as fantastic as their little shops. I love New York City, and some of the work I've done in the past as a writer, producer, and fashion trend forecaster, gives me a great excuse to turn the city over and examine it from the inside out. There is so much to enjoy behind the grand facades of buildings, just around the corner, and even way up on rooftops, beyond what the naked eye can see.

How to use this book

This book is laid out by neighborhood, so wherever you begin your shopping quest, take some time to relax and enjoy the unique energy and spectacle of every New York City block you walk. You'll also find diversions listed along the way—places to eat, drink, and treat yourself—as well as listings for useful services like tailors, cobblers, specific repair shops, and more. Gallery listings are woven throughout different downtown neighborhoods for your enjoyment, since it's nice to balance a shopping day with a little culture. You will find an alphabetical listing of stores in the back of the book as well as an index by shop type.

You'll tour the eclectic East Village, the best in cutting edge home décor and fashion in Williamsburg, trendy Soho and Tribeca boutiques, and the historic Upper East and West Sides. There are some better-known, larger shops mentioned in this book, but for the most part, the focus stays on small shops that reflect a true New Yorker's taste for the best in a city of infinite amusement and amazement. Enjoy!

East Village

The East Village is a neighborhood that knows where it came from, where it's been, and where it's going. Once a part of the Lower East Side, developers renamed the East Village in the 1980s to capture the cachet of historic Greenwich Village and attract new residents. Today, the neighborhood is one of the most eclectic and diverse in the city, and houses the city's oldest and youngest residents side by side. For instance, old folks sit outside of their homes, playing cards, enjoying music and chatting among themselves alongside hip boutiques. Despite the large amount of burgeoning real estate development that's been happening in this area, the neighborhood has retained its downtown, homey feeling, and you're sure to see everything from the century-old to cutting-edge. It's a great neighborhood to do some relaxed shopping and see how New Yorkers really live.

99X

❋ 84 E. 10th Street, bet. 3rd and 4th Aves.
HOURS: Mon–Sat 12-8; Sun 12–7
PHONE: 212-460-8599/8612
WEB: www.99xnyc.com

Where to stock a rocker's wardrobe—the birth-place of British punk style in New York City.

While youths of the last ten years has been crying out for the grit of late '70s and early '80s NYC, 99X has been around since before those babes were wailing. The store opened over twenty-five years ago, and is in its third incarnation (its prior, exotic-sounding location, before 1991, was on East Sixth Street "at the end of a crazy tunnel," says the store's manager). The owner's heritage is British, and she brought punk and ska-influenced brands, like Fred Perry, Doc Marten, Ben Sherman, and Lonsdale stateside—post-Vivienne Westwood and pre-Nirvana. 99X was the exclusive distributor of these now-popular brands for many years, long before American fashion became hip to punk and American department stores began retailing them. Amy Stevons, the store's buyer, tells me the merchandise at 99X, which has always been "pretty much the same," has since come full circle to be coveted by a new generation. 99X could be considered the grandparent (or great-grandparent) of any rough and tumble teen rocker's look today.

You can find vestiges of a bygone punk era in the skinny suits hanging in the back of the store, which the store custom makes for many local musicians. The store space is unobtrusive and far from pretentious. Upon closer examination, there is clearly a great deal of thought behind the buying. Most of the shoes, from classics like Vans to cutting-edge brands like Medium footwear, are limited edition. Vans and other brands do exclusives and higher-end lines for 99X which are not available to major retailers. The store also carries classic shoes like Creepers. Shoe prices range $40–150—which is very reasonable for fashionable sneakers these days.

99X works with many fashion stylists and over the years has become a destination for the discerning punk connoisseur who—tragically—sports Fred Perry in the name of fashion, not ska.

Anna

✳ 150 E. 3rd Street bet. Aves. A and B
HOURS: Mon–Sat 1–8; Sun 1–7
PHONE: 212-358-0195
WEB: www.annanyc.com

Dance-inspired women's clothing that's versatile and sexy.

Kathy Kemp and her shop, Anna, inspired the East Village girl's look in the late '90s: sexy and on the move. Today, Anna thrives by selling dance-inspired, modern clothing with a vintage influence. Kemp, who has designed for Mikhail Baryshnikov's modern dance company, makes clothing that expresses the shape and movement of a woman's body. For instance, a 1999 dress from Anna is a study in curves—a teal tube sheath with a lovely, sheer, stretchy overlaying dress piece that can be rouched and tied and scrunched. Anna's flattering creations boast novel details.

"I like to stay feminine and body conscious, without being too trendy," Kemp told me. She stocks basics, making her like a downtown Donna Karan. Standards include a tight-fitting trench coat that works well for different shapes and sizes; striped faux wrap dresses that tie with ribbon sashes that "are sexy but not too sexy"; and wovens, such as masculine/feminine suiting that compliment a woman's curves. She designs pants with the idea that they can be worn with heels or rolled up and worn with flats—embodying the day to night lifestyle so many young working women have in this city.

"Lots of the pieces I make can be worn a lot of different ways," she says. In fact, one seven-way top/dress, made of silk ($199), comes with an instructional booklet. Since Kemp does extremely limited production runs (she adds three or more new items every week) she uses luxe fabrics from Italy, such as super-soft wool, ultra-soft cotton shirting, silk, and more. Anna also carries jewelry and accessories by her favorite local designers. If all of this doesn't sound like enough of a reason to hightail it down to the East Village, Kemp has a melting pot (literally, a basket) of vintage items, always $20 or less, to mix and match with her designs. The rest of the clothes range from $50–250 (most are priced around or below $100); the trench coat is $350; and the jewelry ranges from $85–150.

John Derian Co.

❊ 6 E. 2nd Street bet. Bowery and 2nd Avenue
HOURS: Tu–Sun, 12–7; Closed Mon
PHONE: 212-677-3917
WEB: www.johnderian.com

Organic crafting meets modern design in this East Village home and lifestyle boutique.

Walking through John Derian's shop is like taking a stroll through a foliage-covered backyard path that winds and twists past exquisite birdbaths and other beautiful decorative objects. Derian has been doing découpage—cut paper on glass—for over 14 years, and carries his line of dishes and house wares in the store. (Dishes range from $400–500.) His work has earned him a serious cult following and made him a darling of the fashion press. Derian's latest work, as well as more information about the art of découpage, can be found on his website. Much of his merchandise is 19th-century European-inspired, but there is a lively and organic feeling of color, texture, and nature in the space as well. Amid the many handmade knickknacks, Derian features numerous pieces of one-of-a-kind artwork for sale, by international and local artists. At John Derian Dry Goods, located two doors down (10 E. 2nd Street), you'll find antiques, textiles, and fine art. Textiles folded and draped all over the store emphasize the idea of being cozy at home. Featured textile designers include Lisa Corti, who uses hand-block printed textiles from India in her collection, and Elsa C. who makes home textiles that marry Age of Enlightenment prints with modern cotton fabrics. Quilts range from $240–1200 in price, while pillows are $55–200. Moroccan lanterns and leather poufs ($200) throw a pinch of spice into the mix. In this second space, Derian features the artwork of British artist Hugo Guinness, who makes original collages and woodblock prints on paper ($350–1100.) Wholesale customers can buy both his and the imported designs online.

Blue

※ 137 Avenue A, bet. St. Mark's Place and
E. 9th Street
HOURS: Mon–Fri 12–7; Sat–Sun 12–5; and by
appointment
PHONE: 212-228-7744

Elegant but unconventional custom wedding and evening gowns by innovative, spunky veteran East Village designer.

The effortless style and charm of Greek-born designer Christina Kara are evident in her dresses, which catch the eye from the street. (In fact, several passers-by stopped and gawked while she fitted a cream strapless dress with a tight box pleat detail in the front on a mannequin.) Kara fell into her profession organically, having started out making cocktail dresses for friends, then eventually buying the shop almost fifteen years ago (which, in today's East Village, is a couple of lifetimes.) Kara's dresses are certainly elegant, but they aren't conservative. "It's not that my dresses aren't balanced, but I want to capture the spirit of the moment," she says. Her dresses are elegant and balanced, but adventurous details—ruffles, hand-textured fabric, ribbons, and an unfinished edge—are what make them stunning. She also carries a breathtaking jewelry line made exclusively for Blue. The pieces are designed for brides, but if you like baubles like I do, you won't wait until your wedding to pick them up. Find Mediterranean-inspired colors and stones like lapis blue and amethyst purple. Jewelry ranges from $80–100; dresses start at $500 and go up to $4,000.

Exceptional Cleaners

These cleaners specialize in couture and bridal, and as such will do a great job with the jeans you refuse to put in the washing machine. They are on the expensive side, but are the best in the city.

Madame Paulette, 1255 Second Avenue, bet. E. 65th and E. 66th Sts., open Mon–Fri 7:30–7, Sat 8–5, 212-838-6827.

Chris French, 57 Fourth Avenue, at the corner of E. 9th Street, open Mon–Fri 7:30–7, Sat 8–5, 212-475-5444.

Need a memorable wedding gift?

There are the shops you know you can find something practical and sturdy—then there are other shops where possibilities you didn't know of exist. Why not make your gift shopping experience feel like less of a chore?

Here are a couple of surefire places to find unusual gifts for your bride- or groom-to-be friends, from high-end to style-end.

Tiffany & Co. (Fifth Avenue at 57th St., 212-755-8000, Personal Shopping: 888-546-5188. Open Mon–Fri, 10–7, Sat 10–6, Sun 12–5). I suppose no shopping guide would be complete without at least one mention of the classic jewelry store made famous by Audrey Hepburn in 1961. It hasn't lost any of its charm—if anything designers at Tiffany's continuously infuse the brand's classic, silver sensibility with fresh new ideas and trends. Tiffany gifts are still as timeless as the film.

At **Moss**, downtown, you can find housewares and gadgets that that transform simple experiences in the home into wondrous moments—objects float, shimmer, and stimulate the senses in ways that a traditional China set may not. Here you can find a conical cheese grater, a neon green wine rack, and a German-designed champagne whisk (to de-bubble the bubbly) that delicately unfolds, like foil from chocolate. See p. 20 for more information.

And, for an international experience, whether you're shopping for a bride or for some unique items to spice up your home décor . . .

Neera Saree Palace (131 Lexington Ave bet. 28th and 29th Sts., Daily 11–7:30, 212-481-0325). Have a Bollywood moment. Find bolts of saree fabrics, blouses, traditional Indian outfits, jewelry, and more.

Butala Emporium (37-46 74th St., Jackson Heights, 718-899-5590). Whether you're Indian or love Eastern-inspired things, find traditional Indian candleholders in terracotta and silver, lanterns, incense holders, small idols, and other tchotchkes for use in ceremonies and centerpieces.

True Love Wedding Center (4876 Broadway at W. 204th St., 212-625-1017). Traditional Chinese wedding dresses, photography, and invitations.

Gomi

❈ 443 East 6th Street bet. 1st Avenue and Avenue A
HOURS: Sun 12–8:30; Mon–Thu 1–8:30; Fri 1–9; Sat 12–9
PHONE: 212-979-0388
WEB: www.gominyc.com, www.myspace.com/gominyc

A small, cool eco-boutique serves up big East Village retail therapy and solutions.

Owner Anne Bernstein, who says she "was hardly political in college" has found her own unique way to educate consumers about the environment with Gomi. The intimate boutique (Gomi means "trash" in Japanese) carries eco-friendly clothing lines, accessories, and gifts. "In New York we have a lot of consumption going on, so I want to create viable alternatives for people without beating them over the head," she says. There's nothing pedantic about Gomi. It's very "East Village" and Bernstein caters to the local consumer, specializing in the most fashion-forward, eco-friendly lines she can find, like Park + Vogel, Prairie Underground, Majestic and Majestic Pure, Vanessa Barrantes, and many more (check the website for prices; you can also shop the collection online). She and her extremely cool and helpful employees impart tidbits of knowledge (for instance, did you know processing bamboo for use in clothing is hard on the environment?) that they hope will help people make educated choices. Gomi is like the dessert course to the documentary film *An Inconvenient Truth*, proving that you can be fun, well-dressed, and socially conscious all at once—without waving a single flag.

Girly NYC

✣ 441 E. 9th Street bet. Avenue A and 1st Avenue
HOURS: Daily 12–7; closed Tu
PHONE: 212-353-5366

Fun, glamorous, retro-influenced lingerie and nightwear by a former T-shirt designer.

It's evident from the logo on the window of the store that "Girly NYC" isn't as straightforwardly precious as it sounds— there is something glamorous, retro, and definitely frisky in the curves of the type. Pam Atwood started designing lingerie after quirky T-shirt designs became commonplace. Her first line of underwear featured James Bond girls silk-screened onto sexy panties, and her sense of humor has only become more refined. Every girl who grew up in the '70s and '80s will appreciate the nod to negligees of those eras in the fabrics and details (small rosebuds and bows) she uses; but the cuts and the styles, which recall Janet and Chrissy of *Three's Company*, have been updated.

Atwood's East Village shop has been around for four years and counting. She was clearly ahead of her time as the lingerie market has simply exploded, and she acknowledges that by carrying other popular lines, like Princess Tam Tam ($35–95), Honeydew ($9–50), Mary Green ($12–175), Playful Promises (from London), Lucy b. (a cute pin-up style line from Los Angeles—$18–65), and much more. Personally, I will always be true to Girly, Atwood's line, which combines fun, sexy, and comfortable into one package. Her lingerie separates are made mostly from nylon and cotton, but the colors and the lace trim are what make them special. She uses brights, like orange, teal, violet, and dark periwinkle, as well as pastels, like sea foam green and pastel pink. Most of the panties are unconstructed bikinis and thongs cut low and straight across; the bras are all of the triangle variety. Look for unusual, retro-inspired nightwear and super-soft cotton jersey negligees.

For the girl in need of her beauty sleep, Girly also carries silk sleep masks ($18–26) and other beauty products; candles from Mor ($36); soaps ($16–20); as well as great jewelry, beautiful cards & small accessories. Panties start at $16, bras at $35, camisoles at $54, and some of the specialty items start at $45 and up.

Frilly, sweet nothings

Tired of the sterile, badly lit, messy, and generally unsavory lingerie sections at most department stores? High-end, pretty lingerie has made its mark as the new shoe as far as sexy accessories go. At **Henri Bendel** (712 Fifth Avenue, bet. W. 55th and 56th Sts., 800-HBENDEL, open Mon–Sat 10–8, Sun 12–7), look for a high-end lingerie department devoted entirely to young, hot new lingerie designers catering to young women with a little extra cash to burn.

Downtown, at discount giant **Century 21** (22 Cortlandt Street, 212-227-9092, open Mon–Fri 7:45–8, Sat 10–8, Sun 11–7); find beautiful stockings and lingerie (designers vary depending on what they get.) A friend swears by the **NY Stocking Exchange** (76 Nassau St, bet. John and Fulton Sts., 212-233-4116), which has a bargain-basement feeling, but actually stocks reputable lingerie brands, like the extremely popular Cosabella.

Back in the East Village, at **Azaleas** (223 E. 10th Street, bet. 1st and 2nd Aves., Tu–Fri 1–8, Sat 12–8, Sun 1–6, closed Mon, 212-253-5484, www.azaleasnyc.com), find a super selection of reasonably priced bras and panties, garters, slips, swimwear, dresses, and more. Azaleas carries more than thirty lingerie designers (see the website for a complete listing,) including Belabumbum, La Cosa, On Gossamer, Woo, and Hanky Panky thongs.

At **Only Hearts** (230 Mott Street bet. Prince and Spring Sts., open Mon–Sat 11–7, Sun 12–7, 212-431-3694), designer Helena Stewart originated the mesh lingerie craze (knocked off by brands like On Gossamer and Cosabella), and her line sticks to it. You can buy boy shorts and bikinis in Delicious (a nylon/Lycra blend) or mesh, trimmed in lace, for $18–40. The standard colors are white, birch, and black, in addition to seasonal colors. The bras are cool too, very reminiscent of a first bra—triangle tops that are soft and comfortable, in mesh or second skin. The shop also sells Stewart's romantic velvet blazers and coats, ultra-feminine skirts, and pliable crewneck mesh shirts, in rich jewel tones like burgundy, ruby, and turquoise. The tops sell for under $100, and the pants and jackets start at $200 and up. (Also located uptown at 386 Columbus Avenue, bet. W. 78th and W. 79th Sts., 212-724-5608, open Mon–Sat 11–8, Sun 11–6.)

Mixona (262 Mott Street, bet. E. Houston and Prince Sts., 646-613-0100, open daily 11–7), features ultra-sexy dressing rooms draped in crimson red silk that are spacious enough to accommodate a guest while you try on the crème de la crème of saucy lingerie by La Perla, Christian Stott, Ravage, La Cosa, and more.

Down in Soho—way down—**Agent Provocateur** (133 Mercer Street, bet. Prince and Spring Sts., 212-965-0229, open Mon–Sat 11–7, Sun 12–6) makes the wickedest, most beautiful lingerie you've ever seen in their bordello of a boutique. The designers, John Corre (Vivienne Westwood's son) and his wife, Serena Rees, have designed different lines of lingerie for different occasions—from flirty to downright naughty scenarios (whips cost $225.) The panties and bras are exquisitely crafted—my favorite was a bra with a silk fringe that hangs across the breast (called Jolene—all of the "ranges," as they are called, have pin-up girl names.) Bras range from $100–170. If you are in the market for super flattering, luxurious undergarments and have some cash to spend, there's no store in the city that will make you feel (or look) hotter than Agent Provocateur.

Toys in Babeland (43 Mercer Street, bet. Broome and Grand Sts., 212-966-2120, open Mon–Sat 12–9, Sun 12–7). This shop runs the gamut, from sex toys to empowerment! The owners, Claire Cavanah and Rachel Venning, opened the store to create an environment that promotes and celebrates sexual vitality in all women. Both Babeland shops attempt to create a positive environment, and their pro-woman, pro-sex outlook has been infectious for women of all ages, as well as couples. The Soho store is a large, open space that rivals any along the same block. Toys you will find at the shop are colorful and interesting—with descriptions to match. It's a fun shop to browse, and you wouldn't believe how cute these toys can be—technology and design have been put to good use here! Visit the website for more information about the company, the merchandise (they do mail-order), and a blog. Also located on the Lower East Side (the original store) at: 94 Rivington St., bet. Ludlow and Orchard Sts., 212-375-1701, open Mon–Sat 12–10, Sun 12–7.

While you're in the East Village . . .

Check out the **Russian and Turkish Baths** on E. 10th Street (268 E. 10th Street, bet. 1st and 2nd Aves., 212-473-8806), which opened in 1892. Wow! Take a walk on the old (and steamy) side, by visiting this East Village institution. For a mere $25, you can spend the day at these aged and surprisingly well-preserved bathhouses. Towels and locks are provided, and there are women-only and men-only mornings during the week (the rest of the times are co-ed).

The entire lower level of the building is the bath, with enclosures for Russian and Swedish sauna rooms (the difference is steam versus dry heat, respectively). There is a cold dunking pool for when you need a refresher. Once you are all steam-clean, head to a sun deck upstairs. The Russian Baths are an Old World-style experience where men and women of all ages come together to—do nothing! And in New York City, that is a very beautiful thing.

Once you've cleansed your skin, your mind, and your worries away, you can go across the street to **Live Live** (261 E. 10th Street, bet. 1st and 2nd Aves., 212-505-5504), a shop that sells locally made raw snacks and munchies, potions and lotions and oils, raw food cookbooks (recommended), and other literature about the raw food movement. For a total day-long experience, end with dinner at **Quintessence** (263 E. 10th St., 646-654-1804) a gourmet raw food restaurant that features entrees and desserts made entirely from raw ingredients. I highly recommend the dessert-as-meal route at Quintessence—you'd be surprised how filling the food is.

Soho

From specialty boutiques to flagships, Soho is the mecca for shopping in New York City. It is one of the most awe-inspiring and historically rich neighborhoods in the city, but it also houses the most retail per block. Once filled with fabric warehouses, printing houses, and artists' lofts, Soho has become one of the most heavily trafficked neighborhoods downtown, especially on weekends. New Yorkers lament its transformation, but don't miss out on the fantastic shopping Soho has to offer. The scene is colorful and lively, from street vendors and artists, to pedestrians walking by.

Most major brands have stores in Soho now—Bloomingdale's opened a downtown location to cater to a younger customer (504 Broadway, Mon–Fri 10–9, Sat 10–8, Sun 11–7, 212-729-5900), as well as hip favorites H&M and Uniqlo. Highlights include the Apple computer store (103 Prince Street bet. Mercer and Greene Sts., Mon–Sat 10–8, Sun 9:30–7, 212-226-3126), which on any given day is brimming with people playing with gadgets, visiting one of the seminars upstairs, or just people watching. If you aren't a Mac user, you may become one after checking out the amply spaced out displays of computers, peripherals, and electronics.

Stores which have outposts in addition to Midtown 5th Avenue flagships include Louis Vuitton, Burberry, Prada, Miu Miu, Emporio Armani, Joseph, Max Mara, Michael Kors, DKNY, Polo by Ralph Lauren, and many more. Most of these stores line the five to six blocks going west from Broadway to Sixth Avenue, along Prince and Spring Streets. You can easily kill four or five hours browsing, shopping, and watching the beautiful people walk by.

Moss

✳ 146 & 150 Greene Street
HOURS: Mon–Sat 10–7; Sun 12–6
PHONE: 212-204-7100
WEB: www.mossonline.com
Gallery located at 152 Greene Street

Industrial design mecca that caters to aficionados and curious passersby with a sumptuous collection of housewares, furniture, appliances, books, and more.

Moss is like a museum of contemporary industrial design, having started as a gallery space in Soho in 1994. Merchandise ranges from the practical—a pocketknife, a clock radio—to the outrageous, such as an oblong, blue and silver, tweed lip-shaped sofa retailing for $13,000. Interesting objects abound, and the staff is knowledgeable and friendly. If the sofa isn't in your budget, check out the books at the southern end of the store—they have a terrific selection of artist monographs and other design/architecture tomes, including works on Bruce Mau, Jasper Morrison, and more. In late 2004, Moss expanded its reach into the ground floor of the luxury condominium building on the corner of Greene and E. Houston Street, to host art shows and other in-store events.

Galleries in Soho

Whether you're in the market for a great piece of art or not, it's fun to add a dash of art and culture to your shopping day in Soho. A shortlist of a few great Soho galleries:

The Drawing Center (35 Wooster Street, 212-219-2166), and **Spencer Brownstone Gallery** (39 Wooster

Street, 212-334-3455), side by side, are two of the best. They feature up-and-coming artists who specialize in politically charged illustrations and drawings.

The Visionaire Gallery (11 Mercer Street, 212-274-8959) is home to the notoriously decadent fashion magazine *V* and collector's edition Visionaire books. They mostly show photography and designer objects.

Avant-garde art dealer Jeffrey Deitch shows a wide variety of artworks at the smaller of his two galleries, **Deitch Projects** (76 Grand Street, 212-343-7300). Deitch's roster is varied, from conceptual street artists to sculpture, dance, and performance. The gallery shows usually reflect the current trend in artwork that references entertainment, technology, and pop culture.

Eye Candy

�֎ 329 Lafayette Street bet. Bleecker and Houston Sts.
HOURS: Mon–Sun 12–8
PHONE: 212-343-4275
WEB: www.eyecandystore.com

Dazzling array of vintage, estate, and new costume jewelry and accessories, including handbags and sunglasses.

The day I visited Eye Candy, I trailed Gwen Stefani up Broadway, where she was shopping with her entourage. Ms. Stefani, who exemplifies how a classic look and modern style can clash to perfection, would probably love the glittery goodness of Eye Candy, a comprehensive new and vintage jewelry shop. When the store opened ten years ago, there were not as many accessories-only stores. Eye Candy still stands out as a destination for the jewelry fanatic.

"It's yin and yang with vintage and fashion. All the design-ers are in here because vintage looks inspired them six months before we see their lines," owner Ron Caldwell told me. He buys vintage jewelry that has a modern feel, and can be mixed with everyday clothes. The pieces in the store are unusual, bright, and colorful, if not downright fabulous. If you are looking for a little sass, and flash, this is a great place to visit. What's fun about the shop is that new pieces are mixed in with the vintage, so you never know what you are getting into until you check out the price tag. In this sense, Eye Candy definitely brings the modern shopper up to speed in vintage accessories.

The shop sells handbags and sunglasses, as well as jewelry. Vintage jewelry ranges from $50-300; new pieces are $20–150; other accessories are $40–300.

Not just jewelry: baubles to party in!

Sometimes, you're looking for something to spice up a simple dress, sweater, or skirt. You want fun but sophisticated jewelry without a high-end price tag, but Forever 21 isn't cutting it. With the resurgence in popu-larity of costume jewelry, here are some party jewelry manufacturers who tastefully knock off vintage styles from the 1970s and '80s.

Girlprops.com (153 Prince Street, at the corner of West Broadway, 212-505-7615. Also in the East Village at 33 E. 8th Street, bet. University Place and Broad-way). Judging from the outside of Girlprops.com, you'd never think that you could find something passable for a woman over 15—the awning is striped in a zebra pat-tern, and the lettering looks like something straight out of *Tiger Beat* magazine. Don't let the initial glare of glit-ter deceive you, though—all along the walls and inside the hundreds of bins at this small downstairs boutique, you will find all kinds of well-made, low-cost costume hair accessories, earrings, necklaces, and more. Granted, if you have a teen in your life, she will love it here too. Nonetheless, who said that you have to be 11 to appreciate hair barrettes and clips shaped like jeweled butterflies and other mythical creatures, beads of all shapes and sizes, and brooches galore? There are accessories in all shapes and sizes, for all hair types and ages.

Marc by Marc Jacobs (403 Bleecker Street, at the corner of W. 11th Street, 212-924-0026, open Mon–Sat 11–7, Sun 12–6). You might be wondering what Marc Jacobs is doing under the "Queen of Costume Jewelry" shop. It's because his shop in the Meatpacking District has great gumball machines that dispense accessories located at the front of the store. You don't have to go into the shop to get to them. Inside the clear bubbles are brooches, rings, and necklaces that are ready to wear. So, you might have spent $3000 on a suit, but who needs to know that you only spent fifty cents on the brooch?

Kiosk

95 Spring Street at Mercer Street, 2nd floor

HOURS: Wed–Sat 12–7

PHONE: 212-226-8601

WEB: www.kioskkiosk.com

Globe-trotting proprietor shares knack for finding the shiniest objects in the haystack.

A visit to Kiosk's website immediately introduces owner Alisa Grifo's special blend of quirky charm and über-cool taste.

It's a minimally (but ingeniously) designed site bursting with curiosities from all over the world, and featuring a companion blog teeming with travel tales. Similarly, her "offline" store, occupying one part of a large studio space in Soho, is the modest home for a wide range of ordinary objects endowed with exotic international identities. A laundry list (raincoat, toothpaste, pencil sharpener, brooch, bubble pipe, chalk, notebook, etc.) won't do justice to each object's real intrigue. "The physical store is good for detail-, design-, and object-minded people who want to see the stuff live," says Grifo. A former prop stylist and set designer, Grifo turned her travel bug into a retail mission: Kiosk is the perfect place to look for a gift or curiosity that piques your interest in life around the world.

Grifo brings insatiable, design-hungry New Yorkers bounty from all over the world, from as far off as Japan, Sweden, Mexico, Germany, and beyond. After sharing cool objects from her travels with friends for years, Grifo was persuaded to open her own store. A chance introduction with a like-minded business partner got Kiosk off the ground. Today, Grifo operates the store on her own. The store's more popular items include retro-inspired Japanese stereo headphones ($125) and a reindeer hide (!) from Sweden ($142). Prices range anywhere from $2 for smaller items like pens, stickers, and more, to $400 for more rarefied objects, like home decorations, original artwork, and more.

Zakka

❈ 147 Grand Street bet. Crosby and Lafayette Sts.
HOURS: Mon–Sun 12–7; Closed on Tu
PHONE: 212-431-3961
WEB: www.zakkacorp.com

Bookstore specializing in graphic design and art books, with a special emphasis on Asian pop culture, toys, and graffiti.

This Japanese-owned bookstore calls itself a "shop and space for creators." Japanese artists have pioneered subcultures in art and music, and Zakka compiles and cross-references these movements to perfection. The shop's main-stay is graphic art-related books, as well as new and old titles on contemporary art, architecture, illustration, and design. The bookstore caters to graphic designers, animators, illustrators, and other artists working in a commercial capacity, and the books examine the construction of images and ideas we see every day. Books can go from $20–100.

Additionally, artists like Kaws and others exhibit their work through for-sale products like T-shirts, toys, and other collectibles. Zakka's in-house team designs innovative T-shirts (around $30). The website is comprehensive and fun to browse. If you'd like to research a particular book or other item before visiting the shop, check it out.

Other Awesome Bookstores

New York City is known for its culture and politics, and the starting point for all kinds of debates lies in its bookstores. These stores are great alternatives to chain booksellers.

St. Mark's Bookshop (31 3rd Avenue cor. E. 9th Street, 212-260-7853, daily 10 a.m.–midnight) is legendary for its selection of criticism and art books.

The Housing Works Bookstore and Café (126 Crosby Street bet. Prince and Houston Sts., 212-334-3324, Mon–Fri 10–9, Sat & Sun 12–7) is a great place to go pick up that Russian novel you never finished in college. Read it at your leisure, overlooking picturesque, cobbled Crosby Street. No one will bother you, no one will come collect what you're reading, and you can stay from morning until night.

At **Unoppresive, Non-Imperialist Bargain Books** (34 Carmine Street, bet. Bedford and Bleecker Sts., Mon–Fri 11-10, Sat & Sun 11-midnight, 212-229-0078) in Greenwich Village, find dirt-cheap editions of classics, from the *Bhagavad Gita* to *Catcher in the Rye* to graphic novels. ($3 and up for new books)

Uptown at **Ursus Books and Prints, Limited** (981 Madison Avenue, bet. E. 76th and E. 77th Sts., 212-772-8787, Mon–Fri 10–6, Sat 11–5, closed Sun) find rare, out-of-print, and new art reference books.

Opening Ceremony

✺ 35 Howard Street bet. Crosby and Lafayette Sts.

HOURS: Mon–Sat 11–8; Sun 12–7

PHONE: 212-219-2688

WEB: www.openingceremony.us

Edgy, downtown store with an international roster of fashion and accessories designers.

Competition for most things is fierce in this city, and the owners of Opening Ceremony took up the challenge of presenting their customers with something different. Each season, Humberto Leon and Carol Lim feature a range of international design talents who "compete" against a team of U.S. designers, headed by their own label, Opening Ceremony.

The store concept originated from a shopping trip to Hong Kong, where many vendors sold disparate items out of separate spaces—Humberto and Carol wanted to pull these items together under one roof. The duo was also inspired by the story about the modern Olympic games—its founder Pierre de Coubertin, pulled all of his interests together in a unifying moment with the Olympics. At Opening Ceremony, the result is a selection of merchandise from a rotating cast of international designers, keeping the store's vibe fresh and interesting.

The standing New York design team is led strongly by the signature Opening Ceremony menswear, womenswear, and shoe collections, and includes pieces by Brazilian visionary Alexandre Herchcovitch, local faves Benjamin Cho, Indigo People, Cloak, and more. The boutique also carries the ubiquitous denim line Cheap Monday ($65 a pop) in a variety of washes you can't find elsewhere in the city. Opening Ceremony's line is always fashion forward—dark, simple clothing with clean, straight to round lines—to wear every day. The shoes, in particular, are exquisite—all '20s-, '30s-, and '40s-inspired, round, delicate shapes that offer a fresh (and über fashionable) take on footwear for women (after all, stilettos are so uptown). All the lines in the store demonstrate a commitment to innovation in fabric or design. Prices range from $25–395 for clothing; $200–1200 for coats; and $10–500 for shoes and accessories.

The two owners handpick everything, and as such, "everything is our favorite," says Humberto. You can find the best of the familiar, the strange, and the exclusive, under one roof. Check the site to find out which country's fashion elite will go up against Team Opening Ceremony next.

Nom de Guerre

✳ 640 Broadway, lower level, underground gate entrance at the southeast corner of Broadway and Bleecker Sts.
HOURS: Mon–Sat, 12–8; Sun, 12–7
PHONE: 212-253-2891

Urban-tinged high fashion for men meets limited-edition footwear and artist-designed clothing in an underground gallery space.

There aren't many shops like Nom de Guerre, where fashion meets art and street culture in such perfect synchronicity. This space is modeled after an Army-Navy store, and inhabits the former meeting space of the Black Panthers. The clothes are sleek basics with unexpected details and high-quality finishing. The four owners come from diverse backgrounds in fashion, design, media, and art. They've created a unique multi-label store that utilizes artwork, music, and design, to cater to a particularly fashion-forward urban shopper. The store is kept almost intentionally covert—on the street outside the shop is a sandwich board that says "Copy Shoppe Downstairs," with an arrow pointing down, into the clubhouse.

The in-house label Nom de Guerre, designed by the in-house team, features elegant redesigns of classic streetwear for men. Throughout the collection, utilitarian ideals meet fine finishing, so you end up with a jacket, a hoodie, or a shirt that can easily be worn under a suit or with a pair of jeans. Other designers the store carries are Patrik Ervel, Commes des Garçons, Trickers of London, and APC. The store also carries limited-edition sneakers that you would be hard pressed to find anywhere else in the city. If you are serious about shopping New York City–style, at Nom de Guerre you have it in the palm of your hand—loose, practical, and effervescently stylish.

Blue Jeans

In Soho and Nolita, fashion rules. Billboards and models abound. Fortunately, for the rest of us, fashion has embraced the everyday luxury of denim, and there is a symphony of denim washes and styles available on the market. In New York City, people take their denim very seriously. As such, here are a few boutiques reflecting the many shades along the spectrum.

At **Built By Wendy** (7 Centre Market Place bet. Broome and Grand Sts., 212-925-6538, open Mon–Sat 12–7, Sun 1–6; in Williamsburg at 46 N. 6th St. bet. Wythe and Kent Aves., open daily 12–7, 718-384-2882), find great American/country-influenced shirting and a new line of Wrangler jeans for men and women by the designer (from $150). These are classic blues, cut a bit higher in the waist and straighter in the leg, perfect for tucking into your cowboy boots.

Pricey but reportedly perfect jeans come from denim purveyor **Earnest Sewn** (on the Lower East Side, 90 Orchard Street, at the corner of Broome Street; in the Meatpacking District at 821 Washington Street), who promises an educational adventure in specialized and custom luxury denim.

The **Diesel Denim Gallery** in Soho (68 Greene Street, bet. Spring and Broome Sts., 212-966-5593, open Mon–Sat 11–7, Sun 12–6) features numbered denim collections made both exclusively for the Gallery by Diesel, and by fashion designers collaborating with Diesel, like Karl Lagerfeld. The space is interesting because it is one of a few spaces in Soho that have been recently occupied by fashion, electronics, and even airline companies, in an effort to bridge the gap between the commercialism of the area and the creative community. The space is more about showing artwork than it is about selling jeans. The mix of art and commerce in the space highlights Diesel's funky novelty denim collection that changes from season to season. The jeans are showcased singly, along the wall and a sparse few racks, and on the southern wall, find a rotating art show, organized by an independent curator. Larger-than-life potted plants sit in the middle of the store. If you are interested in limited edition denim, and have long ago tired of the hackneyed styles walking America's streets, the Diesel Denim Gallery is a must-hit shopping spot. Most jeans start at around $200.

A.P.C. (131 Mercer Street, bet. Prince and Spring Sts., 212-966-9685, open Mon–Sat 11–7, Sun 12–6). Owner/designer Jean Touitou sells his signature, chic, understated basics, but the real reason people are addicted to A.P.C. is the denim. His signature jeans are unwashed, untreated, no-frills dark blue jeans in varying rises and lengths (none, it should be noted, go much below the bellybutton) starting at $150. Staff look Parisian-cool, but are American-friendly.

What Goes around Comes Around (351 W. Broadway, bet. Broome and Grand Sts., 212-343-9303, open Mon–Sat 11–8, Sun 12–7) has a great selection of vintage leather, fur, western wear, women's designer clothing, military, and motorcycle collectibles, with belts and boots to match. Pricey, but could be worth it if you find the perfect pair of high-waisted jeans to sashay to the square dance in! Jeans are around $150; other accessories vary depending on vintage.

dusica dusica

⁜ 67 Prince Street, corner of Crosby and Prince Sts.
HOURS: Mon 11–8; Sun 11–7
PHONE: 212-966-9099
WEB: www.dusicadusica.com

Luxurious collection of handcrafted shoes and bags for a true shoe connoisseur, who has an eye for great design at a great price.

Yugoslavian designer Dusica Sacks teamed up with Aleksandra Hahn (formerly of Prada) to open this minimalist Crosby Street boutique. Using soft leather and other fabrics in muted, flesh-inspired hues, the shoes are built with feminine lines and unusual details. Gathered and ruffled leather, peek-toe covers that can be worn over and under the toes, and chiffon ankle ties give the shoes a delicate and abstract quality. Dusica also specializes in tall waterproof cashmere-lined boots, specially fabricated to withstand at least the milder aspects of a New York City winter.

The handbags are unusual as well, with very little hardware to obstruct the flow of leather and fabric in each bag. Certain styles boast multiple uses, and can be carried as a tote or a slouchy shoulder sack, for instance—just by bending the hidden wire in the strap. Sacks' designs are space-mod, for women who appreciate luxurious details, but don't need the status of logos.

The average cost of shoes here is $200–250, but given the solid construction and beautiful materials, they are practical and versatile enough to justify the cost.

Shoe doctors

From better-known designers like NYC's own **Sigerson Morrison** (28 Prince Street, bet. Mott and Elizabeth Sts., 212-219-3893; also Sigerson Morrison accessories around the corner at 242 Mott Street bet. Prince and E. Houston Sts., 212-941-5404; www.sigersonmorrison.com) to the glam of **Hollywould** (198 Elizabeth Street, bet. Prince and Spring Sts., Mon–Sat 11:30–7, Sun 12–5, 212-219-1905, www.ilovehollywould.com), there are so many fabulous shoes to buy in Soho and Nolita. It's a good thing there's an excellent cobbler nearby keeps soles intact. Head over to **Cowboy Boot Hospital** (4 Prince Street, bet. Bowery and Elizabeth Sts., 212-941-9532, Mon–Fri 9–6, Sat 10–5) where you can fix a broken heel or shape up a sole within minutes, if the cobbler isn't too busy. Prices are reasonable (under $30/pair for most services), and you can talk him down a few dollars depending on how severe the damage is.

Here are the names of some other excellent cobblers around the city, depending on what neighborhood you find yourself in when the sidewalk gets the better of your heel:

Magic Watch and Shoe Repair, (30 Carmine Street, bet. Bleecker Street and 7th Avenue South, 212-

727-2948, Mon–Fri 8–6:30) is my equivalent of a "shoe Nazi" a la *Seinfeld*. He's been known to scold customers for waiting too long before coming in to have the protective Vibrim soles and heel protectors put onto their fancier shoes and boots. ($25/pair)

Alex Shoe Store (57 2nd Avenue, bet. 3rd and 4th Sts., 212-533-9442, Mon–Thu 9–7, Fri and Sun 10–4, closed Sat). These proficient cobblers make platforms for shoes, fix zippers, and the store sells shoes, socks, and other accessories that may have gone the way of your broken heel.

Angelo's (666 Fifth Avenue, at 53rd Street, 212-757-6364, Mon–Fri 7–6:30, Sat 10–5, closed Sun). Major department stores, like Bergdorf Goodman, send their customers to Angelo's. The cobblers specialize in custom work, including matching the fabric of shoes or handbags in order to make alterations or repairs, and dying shoes to match a dress. More famously, the cobbler does boot alterations, including widening with zippers, or tapering baggy knee-high leather boots, to fit them to all sizes of calves. The average cost for boot alteration is $65 and up.

Shoe Service Plus (15 West 55th Street bet. 5th and 6th Aves., 212-262-4823, Mon–Fri 7–7, Sat 10–5). An excellent cobbler who repairs shoes and also dyes shoes to match, which is great for weddings and other special occasions.

Top Service (845 7th Avenue bet. 54th and 55th Sts., 212-765-3190, Mon–Fri 8–6, Sat 9–3, closed Sun). According to some New Yorkers, this is the best place in the city to go have shoes repaired or cleaned. They have been open for fifteen years and for this level of experience are very reasonable. Cleaning costs $6–12, and repair generally doesn't go over $30.

Kaufman Shoe Repair Supplies (346 Lafayette Street bet. Bond and Bleecker Sts., 212-777-1700, open Sun–Fri 6:30–2 a.m.). This store sells missing pieces for broken shoes—heels, tassels, ties, straps, etc.

In God We Trust

❄ 265 Lafayette Street bet. Prince and Spring Sts.
HOURS: Mon–Sat 12–8; Sun 12–7
PHONE: 212-966-9010
135 Wythe Avenue bet. North 7th and 8th Sts.
HOURS: Tu–Fri 1–8; Sat 12–8; Sun 12–7; Closed Mon
PHONE: 718-388-2012
WEB: www.ingodwetrustnyc.com

Influential, independent clothing and accessories designer's vision steals the show in two boroughs.

In God We Trust, the definitive Williamsburg boutique, opened its doors to the Soho shopping crowd in early 2007 to rave reviews. Both spaces reflect owner Shana Tabor's home-spun, ultra-hip sensibility that's clearly influenced style mavens from Bedford Avenue to Bleecker Street. The Williamsburg store is the older sibling of the IGWT family, and compares in size, but is "filled with nooks, and it's an older space, so it feels very Brooklyn," according to Tabor. A Saturday afternoon visit to the Soho store reveals loads of strategically casual, well-heeled young shoppers. The space boasts a polished enclo-sure, with high-ceilings and a bright space. Vintage furniture, ornate mirrors, and cozy closeted racks mingle with animal skins and plants to give one the sense of having stumbled into a fashionable wilderness lodge.

Tabor could probably relax with the success of her In God We Trust clothing label and jewelry line alone (both

made in NYC; jewelry also available at **Catbird**, p.68). However, she shows no signs of stopping with the two boutiques
that house not only her handiwork, but also the work of local
artists like M. Carter (men's and women's T's and sweatshirts);
Shara Porter (silk-screened vintage accessories); and Sover-
eign Beck (eye-catching men's ties of original designed silks
made in NYC, for around $100); as well as LA-based Kristen
Coates (women's dresses) and Australian label Ritten House
(men's sweaters and sweatshirts). "Ironically, I like it when
other designers are doing something similar [to In God We
Trust]," says Tabor, "or, if it's just something I would like to
wear myself." Dresses range from $220–280; fine jewelry from
$80–300; and men's shirts from $240–260.

Amarcord

❖ 252 Lafayette St. bet. Prince and Spring Sts.

HOURS: Mon–Sat 11–7:30; Sun 12–7

PHONE: 212-431-4161

223 Bedford Avenue, Williamsburg, Brooklyn bet. N. 4th
and N. 5th Sts.

HOURS: Daily 12–8

PHONE: 718-963-4001

WEB: www.amarcordvintagefashion.com

Outlet location: 84 E. 7th Street, bet. 1st and 2nd Aves.

HOURS: Tu–Sun, 12–7:30, closed Mon

PHONE: 212-614-7133

*Pristine Italian vintage clothing and accessories
for high-fashion lovers.*

The luxury, glamour, and style of modern Italian film is alive
and well at this bastion of European vintage clothing and
accessories. Named eponymously for the famous Fellini

movie, Amarcord's owners passionately evoke the die-hard connection between fashion and the immortal moving image. Owners Marco Liotta and Patti Bordoni are both vintage veterans, having spent years selling at the flea markets in Chelsea (p. 63). Bordoni grew up in fashion in Italy, where his grandfather was a tailor. The clothing, shoes, and handbags at Amarcord are nothing short of exquisite. Everything is color-coded and in phenomenal condition—Sophia Loren-style Italian knits, trench coats, skirts, and dresses hang impeccably like pristine relics. Amarcord carries some new designers, such as the Italian accessories designers Roberta di Camarino and Sergio Rossi. Their vintage selection includes rare Gucci bags, Dior, YSL, Celine, and Missoni. Taking a cue from Fellini, there's great humor in Liotta and Bordoni's choices: patent yellow leather and Lucite details, flat metallic and gold accents, and anything that's of the moment in fashion today.

Prices vary widely depending on the item—the average cost of shoes is $150, handbags average around $200, and clothing starts at $30, depending on the item.

Note there are two other store locations: the Williamsburg location, and an outlet store in the East Village that has some serious finds. The couple also owns a vintage warehouse worthy of any starlet's wildest costume fantasies. Located near the Williamsburg shop, the gargantuan facility houses 16,000 pieces which are not for sale, but available for viewing by appointment. Call the Williamsburg location for details.

Nolita

Nolita (a hybrid moniker of "North of Little Italy") is known for its quaint buildings, leafy streets, and small boutiques. In the last ten years, the neighborhood has become a hub for younger designers and shops that carry cutting-edge clothing and accessories. However, the Old World romance of the neighborhood, once home to Martin Scorsese and other legendary Italian-American New Yorkers, remains. Most of the stores' employees reflect the current feeling of the neighborhood—youthful, relaxed, and beautiful. Nolita combines the quality of Soho shopping with the chill vibe of the Village—without the crowds. A great part of town to grab a seat at an outdoor café and people watch, because it doesn't get prettier than this.

No. 6

✽ 6 Centre Market Place bet. Broome and Grand Sts.
HOURS: Tu–Sat 12–7; Sun 12–6
PHONE: 212-226-5759
WEB: www.no6store.com

Former fashion stylists tempt weak-willed shoppers with to-die-for vintage clothing and accessories from every era and their own neo-vintage dress label.

No. 6 is tucked away on a special, cobbled Manhattan street that dwindles off after just a couple blocks, which makes finding it feel like stumbling onto hidden treasure. This elegant shop opened just a couple of years ago, and has quickly expanded to carry not only beautiful American and European vintage, but also excellent independent designers and a house line called No. 6. The store has a powerful team behind it: Morgan Yakus and Karin Berenson, both former fashion stylists, who happily and graciously lend their styling cred from the fashion and advertising worlds to dressing each one of us. And what an extremely personal experience it is—Berenson shares tales of customers feeling so comfortable in the store that they undress right there, and stay for hours just to hang out. "This is a place where people can go even if they don't know much about vintage and fashion," says Yakus. Customers become fast friends with each other, and with the store's proprietors, whom they'll often phone to report their ecstatic shopping triumphs. ("We have no problem telling people to go home and think about it. I've been known to cut people off, even," says Berenson.) It was this personal touch—expert styling and tailoring suggestions—that quickly blossomed into the house label. "We would hand-alter dresses to make our customers their dream vintage dress," says Berenson. "For instance, if they loved a dress from the fifties, but wished it was a little shorter . . . things like that." Barney's quickly found out about what the two were doing for customers and placed "a massive, ridiculous order." The line was met with much success, and the label has continued on, evolving each season from altered vintage, to original designs in vintage fabrics, to new design with new fabrics. Berenson describes the several styles of dresses on offer as ones that women can just live in, 24/7. "You could dress it up or down. You could wear it in winter or summer. Everyone who buys our dresses say they wear them every day and get a million compliments." No. 6 dresses range in price from $20–315; the store also carries Staerck, Electric Feather, shoes by B Store from London, and crochet necklaces by wunderkind Arielle de Pinto. Berenson describes the store's atmosphere as "the essence of change. Whether it's the walls, the floors, the upholstery on the sofa, or new merchandise, our customers can always find something new and feel right at home every time they come in." There's something comforting about a rock like No. 6 in the ever-changing sea of fashion, helmed by two such dedicated captains.

The Good the Bad & the Ugly

❖ 85 Kenmare Street at Mulberry Street
HOURS: Mon–Sat 11–7; Sun 12–7
PHONE: 212-473-3769
WEB: www.goodbaduglynyc.com

Veteran downtown designer enjoys cult following with her signature denim line and more at this laid-back boutique

Judi Rosen (whose dresses you can find at **Honey in the Rough** p. 78) is a popular downtown New York designer and proprietor. GBU spokeswoman Stephanie Hodge describes Rosen as a wholly self-taught designer and patternmaker, who is "insanely crafty. She'll come into the store and build shelves in her high heels and minidress." Once an East Village staple, GBU has resided on the edge of Nolita since 2006 and poses a challenge to its customers: Will you be able to fit into Rosen's wait-listed (Barney's is a suitor), to-die-for, high-waisted style denim? Yes, says Hodge: "The type of woman Judi designs for is a really curvy woman." Her designs reflect this. The pants come in two styles—a cigarette, which runs long and skinny (and, Hodge adds, were available at GBU way before the skinny silhouette was in vogue) and the "elephant belle" style, which are "really traditional '70s bell-bottoms that start at the top of the thigh." Whoo-wee. Because there is a new collection every season that varies in fabric and not insignificant details (the pocket, yoke, rise, etc.), the demand for Rosen's pants remains high. Thus the pants ($190–225) are legitimately collectible, being made in NYC, produced in a very small run, and selling out the second they arrive—twice a year. GBU also carries men's denim, as well as dresses, accessories, gloves, tights and socks—all in line with Rosen's vision. Her excellent sense of humor and dedication are sure to resound with generations of pretty young things for years to come.

Malia Mills

※ 199 Mulberry Street, bet. Spring and Kenmare Sts.
HOURS: Mon–Sun, 12–7
PHONE: 212-625-2311
WEB: www.maliamills.com

Swimsuit boutique that makes flattering cuts for any body type in fashion-forward fabrics and unusual, fun colors.

Malia Mills has a loyal clientele who pay homage to her boutique year after year. Why? Because Malia has almost succeeded in shattering the barrier between women and their bodies with her suits. It's hard to believe that liberation for women and their curves would come from a swimwear designer. However, Malia has made it her company's mission to take the edge off of bathing suit shopping—which is a tall order. She pulls it off by cutting flattering shapes, pushing the envelope with novel fabrications and embellishments, and creating a positive store environment. Her company's motto is "Love Thy Differences."

The store is simple—a rack of suits on the right, a long chest of drawers on the left. The staff is friendly and will find you your size, make color suggestions, and smile all the while. The dressing rooms are spacious, with room for friends to provide moral support. "We're here to make shopping for swimwear as anxiety-free and liberating as possible," says a spokesperson for Malia Mills. Suits range from $80 per piece, and up. The other cool thing about Malia Mills is that mixing and matching is encouraged, and many of the colors and fabrics complement one another. At the end of each season, the store has a great sale where you can get two pieces for the price of one. Call the office or check the website for details about the sales.

Also uptown at 960 Madison Avenue, bet. E. 75th and 76th Sts. (212-517-7485; open Mon–Sat 10–7)

Daily 235

❊ 235 Elizabeth Street, bet. Prince and Houston Sts.
HOURS: Mon–Sat 12–8; Sun 12–7
PHONE: 212-334-9728
WEB: www.daily235.com

Offbeat gift shop specializing in kitsch and memorabilia.

Daily 235 is a little gift shop that's tucked between two boutiques in Nolita, like a playful puppy sandwiched between a couple of serious adults. The shop has occupied this position on the block for over ten years, long before Nolita was a hip shopping destination. The owner, Jasmine Krause, and her partner once worked for Ad Hoc, a popular and revolutionary home store in Soho in the '80s that pioneered wired shelving and industrial shelving units for the home. Today, Krause and her partner use these shelves in their store, which is a small, spare space, packed with fun toys, gift items, and memorabilia, artfully arranged to invite experimentation.

It's easy to see why the shop is so popular and has been

around for so long. The reasonably priced gift items are both historically and culturally fascinating. The store is a veritable museum for random objects and memorabilia; it could be 2005 or 1920 for all you know. Merchandise includes gag gifts (trick cigarettes and gum, jack-in-the-box), to memorabilia from the '50s, to comic books and toys, to lunchboxes. The nostalgic feeling in the store often gives way to modern humor, and it is always changing. Daily 235 is the perfect place to pick up a last minute gift or something just for fun. Prices are reasonable for the novelty and the neighborhood— you can find something neat for $3.

I got you babe

Kids are little people. Sometimes they get stuck wearing something that's a bit more "appropriate" than they would prefer. Here are some shops that let the young ones reap the same benefits of fun, varied shopping options their parents do. From toys to T-shirts, here are a couple of the coolest babies' and kids' shops in lower Manhattan.

Sons and Daughters (35 Avenue A bet. E. 2nd and E. 3rd Sts., Mon–Tu 12–7, Wed–Sun 10–7, 212-253-7797, www.sonsanddaughtersinc.com) has everything for the coolest mom-to-be you know, from minimally designed all-wood Scandinavian toys (wood's better for baby) and ABC books by graffiti artists to the best eco-friendly kids' clothes.

Dinosaur Hill (306 East Ninth Street, bet. 1st and 2nd Aves., 212-473-5850, open daily from 11–7). Everyone in the East Village loves this eclectic toy store, including parents and overgrown kids like me. You'll find unusual handmade marionettes from the Czech Republic dangling from the ceiling ($21–$90), plus sequined wooden horses from Burma and Thailand and jack-in-the-boxes (cat-, dog-, and cow-in-the-boxes, too). They also have UGLY doll keychains, as well as a variety of stuffed animals. The store stocks many neat toy brands and makes from your childhood that are gratifying to see in the face of Wal-Mart swallowing all the cool toy-makers. Dinosaur Hill also gift wraps everything on the premises, which is a huge time saver as well.

Julian & Sara (103 Mercer Street bet. Prince and Spring Sts., 212-226-1989, open Tu–Fri 11:30–7, Sat–Sun 12–6). A children's clothing store that's a bit on the pricey side, but the bonus is that while you're shopping, your little ones can play with the toys in the store, so you can browse in peace. The store carries an almost entirely European catalog of clothing, with sizes ranging from infants to age 12 (although your 12-year-old may not be so psyched about the clothes in here.) Dresses are unpretentious in ecru and ivory woven fabrics ($100–250). Stop here for a special baby gift, or to indulge your newest family member with something a little extraordinary. Miniature dress shirts and slacks for boys ($100–250) are adorable, if only until next year.

I Heart

✳ 262 Mott Street, bet. Prince and Houston Sts.
HOURS: Mon–Sat 12–8; Sun 12–7
PHONE: 212-219-9265
WEB: www.iheartnyc.com

Immense store and gallery and lounge space featuring local artwork, books, and music, amid collections of cutting-edge women's fashion.

The precious name of this store belies the edginess of its immense subterranean space, with its 17-foot ceilings. Owner Jill Bradshaw is a veteran in New York's creative community and brings a non-traditional yet classy sensibility to her store. Always featuring the artwork of local designers and painters, the space is designed for comfort and play, a station on the dial of cultural frequency. The accessories, books, and CDs are displayed along the wall in glass cases and on modular shelving units, as in an art gallery. Her inspiration comes from art, color, music, and her favorite designers. I Heart's spacious, relaxed atmosphere provides a welcome change from Nolita's shops.

Featured (and pretty consistent, says Bradshaw) I Heart designers include Tsumori Chisato, Karen Walker, Eley Kishimoto, United Bamboo, Wood Wood, Perks and Mini, and Lover. Most of these lines cater to a younger working customer. Eley Kishimoto makes shoes, handbags, and clothes, using bright colors and a combination of contrasting elements like leather and suede, or leather and perforated plastic. United Bamboo's line provides the fashionable professional with quality suiting and luxe detailing. There is a wide range of items, and the prices reflect this spectrum. Tops range from $40–300; bottoms $90–300; coats $150–1000; shoes $50–500; books, CDs and other smaller gift items are $5–50.

There is a lounge area to read books, as well as a listening station to sample the latest musical flavor of the moment. CDs also include compilations by local DJs, generally rock, rap, reggae, or disco.

Where the music is

A great deal of New York's cultural currency stems from the abundance of sources we have for music. Here are the best:

Other Music (15 E. 4th Street bet. Broadway and Lafayette St., Mon–Fri 12–9, Sat 12–8, Sun 12–7, 212-477-8150, othermusic.com). OM has a selected canon of the classics, and they carry many local and hard to find labels and artists from around the world. Electronic, dub, and rock are the forte here. Staff is very knowledgeable and helpful, and the store publishes a great e-mail newsletter full of vivid detail and recommendations. OM also hosts in-store appearances by some of their featured artists—check their website for details.

Etherea (66 Avenue A bet. E. 4th and E. 5th Sts., Sun–Thu 12–10, Fri–Sat 12–11, 212-358-1126, www.ethereaonline.com). A small independent music shop open since 1995. In addition to a great selection of popular and alternative music, Etherea stocks premier imported music magazines, like *The Wire* from the UK. Find a good selection of popular indie artists; if you've recently read about a band, you will find them here easily. I like that Etherea isn't as expensive as Other Music. Most of the CDs are around $13.

Jammyland (60 E. 3rd Street, Mon–Thu 12–8, Fri–Sat 12–10, 212-614-0185, www.jammyland.com). A

Jamaican music store specializing in new, rare and hard to find dub plates, reggae, and dancehall.

Kim's Music and Video (6 St. Mark's Place bet. 2nd and 3rd Aves., Daily 9–12, 212-598-9985, www.mondokims.com). Are you asking everyone you know if they've heard of an album or movie, and no one has? Looking for the complete Kurosawa catalog? Chances are you'll find it at Kim's! The used CDs here are especially good because the store's discerning customers donate them. They also sell vinyl.

Cake Shop (152 Ludlow Streets bet. Stanton and Rivington Sts., 212-253-0060, www.cake-shop.com). Yes, an actual café/bakery with a vegan focus, but really, a music shop. Find vinyl and CDs with a concentration on local music, as well as small press comics and zines, DVDs, magazines, books, and other assorted oddities. Downstairs, a hopping music venue features performances by the best local independent bands.

Selima Optique

❋ 25 Prince Street, bet. Mott and Elizabeth Sts.
  HOURS: Mon–Fri 12–8; Sat 11–7; Sun 12–6
  PHONE: 212-334-8484
  WEB: www.selimaoptique.com

Pioneering fashion specs designer's Nolita boutique offers frames for multiple personalities.

The smallest of eyeglass empress Selima Salaun's eponymous NYC boutiques (one specializes in corsets), the Nolita Selima is surrounded by ever-popular restaurants and cafés (Café Gitane and Café Habana are both a block away), and the store enjoys evening and after-dinner customers who happily peruse Selima's gorgeous eyeglass frames, hats, and other accessories. Selima's frames, which revolutionized fashion eyewear in the 1990s, are handcrafted artisanal plastic in vivid hues. The shapes are Eames-inspired—fluid, quirky, simple—and have names like Fish, Mouth, and Wing. Selima owns eight boutiques in Paris, New York, and Los Angeles. She is big on selling you as many pairs of glasses as she can to suit every one of your adorable personalities.

Eyewear

Selima Optique (84 E. 7th Street bet. 1st and 2nd Aves., 212-260-2495, Daily 12–7:30). Selima's fabulous boutiques can be found all over the city. There must be a frame for everyone—picky or not—in her store.

Also at:

Bond 07 by Selima, 7 Bond Street, bet. Broadway and Lafayette Sts., 212-677-8487, Mon–Sat 11–7, Sun 12–7.

59 Wooster Street, at the corner of Broome Street, 212-343-9490, Mon–Sat, 11–8, Sun 12–7

899 Madison Avenue, bet. E. 72nd and E. 73rd Sts., 212-988-6690, Mon–Sat, 10:30–7, Sun 12–6.

At **Fabulous Fanny's** (335 E. 9th Street bet. 1st and 2nd Aves., Daily 12–8, 212-533-0637), find vintage frames from the designer who made frames for George Washington and Thomas Jefferson, as well as chic costume frames that the shop lends on occasion to theater and film companies involved in costume or period projects. Prices for frames vary widely depending on vintage.

Naked Eye (192 Orchard St. bet. Houston and Stanton Sts., Tu–Fri 1–8, Sat 12–7, Sun 12–6, closed Mon, 212-

253-4935, www.nakedeyeoptical.com). A well-curated selection of frames from Cutler and Gross, Christian Roth, Dita, and many more, showcased in a very Zen-like space. Owner George Lee will most likely be on hand to give you his expert (and personal) opinion, which, as any diehard glasses-wearer will tell you, is invaluable.

Facial Index (104 Grand Street at Mercer St., 646-613-1055, Mon–Sat 11–7, Sun 12–6). This Japanese-owned store features avant-garde, modern frames from all over the world. Prices start at $260 for frames.

Morgenthal Frederics (944 Madison Avenue, at E. 74th St. 212-744-9444, Mon–Fri 10–7, 212-744-9444). This quintessential New York store's delicate, lace-pattern laminates and etched metals stand out from the crowd. Prices vary widely from $200 all the way up to $1,000 for fourteen-carat gold frames.

Gas Bijoux

✣ 238 Mott Street, bet. Prince and Spring Sts.
  HOURS: Mon–Sat 11–7, Sun 12–6
  PHONE: 212-334-7290
  WEB: www.gasbijoux.fr

  French collection of Asian-inspired costume jewelry for the woman who's not afraid of a little sparkle.

Andre Gas, a French designer who owns several boutiques in Paris and St. Tropez, among other places, infuses his jewelry with his cosmopolitan sensibility. Atop the wooden cabinets around the perimeter of the shop are bright green silk brocade panels that elaborate on the jewelry's colonial sensibility. Gas embellishes Asian-influenced beads or coins with glass, rhinestones, or enamel, before incorporating them into his designs. His signature earring shape is the chandelier, which comes in many different colors and shapes. The jewelry has a festive, holiday feel to it, but some pieces are very Bohemian at the same time. You can wear a more elaborate piece to a wedding, or dress anything down with a T-shirt for a night of karaoke. These pieces are imaginative, feminine, and fun, and worth a bit of a splurge. ($145–215)

Street Vendors

Hundreds of different vendors line Broadway, Prince and Spring streets (they're out year-round, but more so in the spring and summertime.) You can find everything from art books, to designed matchbook covers, dolls, curios, and more. For both tourists and natives alike, street vendors are wonderful because the merchandise for sale is handmade, often one-of-a-kind craftwork that would sell for hundreds inside a shop. Buying from these vendors also differs from the more popular flea markets in the city (see Flea Markets, p. 63) because the selection is carefully curated to cater to the discerning shopper.

The streets are the place the find the next big thing in jewelry and crafts design, as many young designers do not have the means to produce their lines commercially. Urban Outfitters will charge you $30 for a pair of earrings you can find (better made) from one of these vendors for $10. Shopping these vendors is a good way to support local artists who have built up a thriving outdoor retail community in Soho. They have established outdoor retail spaces for themselves, and many of them have been in the same licensed location for years. A random sampling of permanent vendors (there are many) include:

There is a vendor on Prince Street who sells round, ample, hand-knit/crocheted, nubby hats and ponchos ($25 and up).

Art, architecture, photography coffee table books: on Prince Street, titles from Taschen, Phaidon Press, and others, sell for 10–30 percent below market value.

Cleo Van Elton, a jewelry designer and vendor who sits on the corner of Prince and Broadway, designs earrings and necklaces using papier-mache with gold overlay, semiprecious stones with sterling silver; and gold-plated sterling silver. Her styles are very feminine and always on trend ($15–100).

The T-shirt peddler on Prince Street between Broadway and Mercer Sts., is also a veteran of the Soho street vendor scene. He screen-prints old movie logos, rock bands, funny sayings, and more, onto American Apparel T-shirts. His T's go for $11 a piece (which is a steal in an oversaturated T-shirt market) but you can negotiate if you buy more than one.

Hand-painted matchbooks, right outside of Mercer Kitchen restaurant, at the corner of Greene and Prince Sts.

Along West Broadway between Houston and Canal streets, you can find many street artists producing original paintings, charcoal drawings, watercolors and sketches, as well as vendors selling photographs. It's quite possible to find a nice piece of original artwork here for under $100.

Zero Maria Cornejo

❋ 225 Mott Street, bet. Prince and Spring Sts.
HOURS: Mon–Fri 1–8; Sat and Sun 12:30–6:30
PHONE: 212-925-3849
WEB: mariacornejo.com
807 Greenwich Street, corner of Jane St.
HOURS: Mon–Sat 12–7, Sun 12–6:30
PHONE: 212-620-0460

Luxe fabrics and elegant, simply designed clothing for style mavens of all ages.

Like its name, Zero starts from the beginning, building elegant, functional pieces from simple designs. The clothing comes in geometric, imaginative shapes in Southwestern taupes, creams, and greys; visually the clothing would be appealing on everyone from a dancer to a woman who is several months pregnant. Capelets, ponchos, wide-leg trousers, pleated skirts, and dresses, fill out Maria Cornejo's versatile collection. On her website are photographs of the current season's line, which will give you a better sense of her aesthetic.

The Chilean-born designer pays a great deal of attention to details and draping of fabric. The idea is to easily incorporate any of her unusual pieces into your everyday wardrobe. Contrast is key to her design; she uses prints with solids, and sharp tailoring with fluent contour. The fabrics are unusual and of high quality, like viscose jersey, silk charmeuse, Scottish wool, French herringbone wool, African jacquards, indigo denim, organic cotton sweatshirt, silk cashmere, shiny lamé, and many more. Cornejo also features a bridge collection made of fleece that includes wraps and cardigans.

Cornejo originally opened the space in 1997 to join the movement of independent designers in New York who use small design studios to manufacture and sell their own lines. Zero is named for its very basic approach to design. The line is sold at Barney's New York, but you'll find the Nolita shop is a cool grey pond compared to the chaos in midtown Manhattan. The space is gallery-like, and the clothing feels like wearable art.

Prices are on the higher side, but for basics like trousers and sweaters, Zero outshines traditional brands like Donna Karan or Ralph Lauren. It's nice to wear a plain piece that isn't completely predictable, but looks elegant. You can buy a T-shirt for $49; pants are generally between $189–289; tops can go anywhere from $189–395, depending on the fabric; coats will run from $600–900; the lower-end fleece collection sells for between $196–240.

Polux Fleuriste

248 Mott Street, bet. Prince and Houston Sts.
PHONE: 212-219-9646
HOURS: Mon–Fri 9–7; Sat 12–7; closed Sun

Flowers from all over the world are transformed into French country-style, artistic arrangements for delivery.

Audrey Tatou loading her bicycle up with wine and flowers on her way home in *Amélie* is enviably representative of the average citizen's life in Paris. Polux owner Anoushka Levy, a Parisian, says she wanted to recreate her hometown's romanticism here in New York. Her flower shop, next door to her husband's superb restaurant Café Gitane, is French down to the very last detail. Her exquisite flower collection comes from all over the world—the Netherlands, Israel, and South America, for starters.

The inside of the store is cool and tiled, and was custom designed to feel like a Parisian shop, all the way to a stone basin in the back with a single gold faucet. Levy has incorporated a lifestyle element into the boutique, and sells handmade teacups and bowls, loose teas, candles, marmalade, dolls made from vintage fabrics, and much more ($20 and up).

The minimum for delivery is $75, but if you visit the store, you can find an arrangement for any price you wish (though it may be small if you go too low.) Polux also incorporates vintage elements into its arrangements, such as an 18th-century vase, jars from the 1940s, and vintage fabrics. With a delivery, Polux includes lovely handmade details in the packaging, like a wax "Polux" seal on the leaf of the flower, a handmade cookie, and flower food that is attached to a small illustrated pamphlet on how to care for your flowers. It's sweet down to the very last touch. Anoushka's sentiment about bringing us the good life is infectious.

While you're there . . .

You may want to walk further south into Chinatown to **Golden City Floral Arts** (221 Centre Street, at Grand St., 212-219-0235) where they have gorgeous orchids, lilies, and tulips for very reasonable prices. They also do decent arrangements quite cheaply, and the old woman who works in here is so charming that the whole experience is very pleasant.

Shopping in Full Bloom

Manhattan's flower district can be intimidating to the first timer, but here are a few shops to check out. Incidentally, another great way to shop in New York is to shop the districts—generally, they are one city block of different stores selling different varieties of the same item. If you have the cash and want flowers for decoration, the selection in the Flower District is exquisite. The Flower District is, roughly, on W. 28th Street between 6th and 7th Aves.—some stores spill onto 6th Avenue as well. Between the hours of 7 and 9 a.m., the shops are filled with stylists, decorators, and designers fiercely competing over the best varieties of flowers available, so don't expect the vendors to be very helpful if you want to buy a lily for your office desk. However, if you go in the middle of the day, you can certainly choose flowers to your liking, that are much nicer than what you will find at your neighborhood deli.

There are stores that specialize in different varieties of flowers—from tropical to country flowers to grasses. Here are several stores in the Flower District worth checking out. They are all markets, and as such the selection changes on a daily basis. They are, however, the largest in the District, so you are sure to find what you are looking for at any one of them:

Fischer & Page Ltd. (134 W. 28th St. bet. 6th and 7th Aves., 212-645-4106, Daily 6 a.m.–11 a.m., Sat open a little later and closed a bit earlier).

Associated Cut Flower Company, Inc. (118 W. 28th St., bet. 6th and 7th Aves., 212-367-7805).

US Evergreen (805 Sixth Avenue bet. 27th and 28th Sts., 212-741-5300, Mon–Fri 5 a.m.–1:30 p.m., Sat 6–1).

Jamali Garden Supplies (149 W. 28th St. bet. 6th and 7th Aves., Mon–Sat 6:30–5, 212-996-5534, www.jamaligarden.com) specializes in floral, garden, and other decorative products from all over the world at wholesale prices. Check their site for details.

Red Flower

❋ 13 Prince Street, bet. Bowery and Elizabeth Sts.
HOURS: Daily 12–7
PHONE: 212-966-5301
WEB: www.redflower.com

When you don't want a run-of-the-mill vanilla candle, Red Flower carries comfort items in specially formulated fragrances from all over the world.

From the great airline-inspired logo to the relaxing dark environs of their Nolita store, Red Flower promises to provide a very cool experience. Yael Alkalay and Victor Silviera, childhood friends who traveled the world over, have put together a collection of soaps, lotions, teas, and candles that give off exotic scents from every corner of the globe. The products are superior because of the purity of fragrance, the simple, elegant packaging, and the fantastic customer service you get when you visit the store. They serve Red Flower's jasmine tea, which you can sip through a bombilla, a metal straw with a round perforated bulb at the bottom, from Argentina (also for sale, $20).

Celebrity patronage is in no short order here, as Madonna swears by the Spanish Gardenia, R&B singer Usher by the Italian Blood Orange, and rumor has it that P. Diddy only burns Himalayan Larch candles in his Manhattan offices.

Prices range from $18–32, making a stop at Red Flower perfect for a gift or for a self-indulgent treat.

Yoga

Some of us indulge in a spiritual massage after a long day of shopping, and inside of the many buildings in lower Manhattan are yoga studios packed with women and men of all ages. Fortunately, most studios offer classes frequently, are not terribly expensive, and offer additional services like massage, fresh food and juices, and more.

Atmananda Yoga & Holistic Spa (324 Lafayette Street bet. Bleecker and E. Houston Sts., 7th Floor, Yoga: 212-625-1511, Holistic Spa: 212-625-1511, www .atmananda.com). Atmananda is known for its teacher-training institute, but it also features a food and drink bar where raw food dishes are featured. Massage, facials, and waxes are also offered. Classes include the Ayangar style of yoga, which is a slow and detailed practice that allows you to focus on getting your postures and movements absolutely correct while focusing on special muscle groups. Classes cost only $10, the cheapest on this list.

Jivamukti Yoga School (841 Broadway, 2nd fl., bet. 13th and 14th Sts, 212-353-0214, 800-295-6814, www .jivamuktiyoga.com). Probably the most "celebrity-fied" yoga center in the city, this popular studio was once frequented by Madonna, and Russell Simmons is on its board. Classes here may be more crowded and expensive, but the instruction is superb. $20 for a single class—get into it.

Bikram Yoga NYC (212-245-2525; various locations; check website for more information; www.bikram yoganyc.com). Bikram is the "hot" style of yoga, where the airtight room is heated up to 100 degrees to allow for optimal stretching conditions. $20 for a single class, although the first week, you can go to an unlimited number of classes for this price.

Greenwich Village/ Meatpacking District

Greenwich Village is generally regarded as a deeply histori-cal and significant neighborhood. A stroll through the Village is breathtaking, particularly the majestic brownstones and quiet, tree-lined streets. There are hundreds of cafes, artisanal shops, galleries, and historic sites to visit. In recent years, the "good life" spread a bit further north to the Meatpacking Dis-trict, a city hot spot bustling with shops, restaurants and bars, and hotels. Meatpacking stores are ideal for finding superb design ideas and objects for the home. A walk through the Village and the Meatpacking District is a must, with shops hiding in corners where you least expect them.

Butik

❖ 605 Hudson Street bet. 12th and Bethune Sts.
HOURS: Tu–Fri 12–7; Sat 11–7; Sun 12–6
PHONE: 212-367-8014
WEB: www.butiknyc.com

Eclectic Greenwich Village shop specializing in Scandinavian fashion and found objects.

Butik (an old-fashioned Danish word that means "specialty store") is the shop of model-slash-photographer (and neighbor-hood resident) Helena Christensen and her lifelong best friend, Danish flower artist, Leif Sigersen. One of the luxuries a super-model's passport affords is a thoughtfully curated international selection of clothing, antiques, candles, lamps, flowers, and chocolates—gathered from frequent travels through Denmark, Sweden, Paris, and beyond. The West Village boutique space, transformed from a bar, delights the imagination with found objects and hard-won elegance—a décor that rivals a Civil War costume drama movie set. High ceilings, exposed brick walls, and French doors are the preserved remnants from the old bar, and a hothouse for flowers at the back of the store separates the retail space from the owners' studio. The clothing is a mix of both new and vintage. The vintage standouts carry through the old military-chic feeling of the store, like refurbished 60s military garb (thermals) that function as everyday staples, as well as comfy, lived-in vintage nightgowns. Designers include Christensen-Sigersen, the airy collaboration between the two owners, and Danish rising star Staerck, among others. Think whimsical, fairytale details crossed with cool Scandinavian nonchalance and you'll get a sense of what the duo gravitates towards. Examples of other oddities that might seduce your eye (the selection changes all the time) include crochet yarn dolls and antique kitchenware. Visit Butik to gauge the inverse ratio between Denmark's fashion destination status, and New York City's uncanny ability to make the unusual completely accessible to anyone who passes by.

Flight 001

❄ 96 Greenwich Avenue at Jane St.
   HOURS: Mon–Fri 11–8; Sat 11–8; Sun 12–6
   PHONE: 212-691-1001
   WEB: www.flight001.com
   58 5th Avenue, bet. Bergen St. and St. Mark's Place
   HOURS: Mon–Sat 11–8; Sun 11–6
   PHONE: 718-789-1001

Hip travel store featuring the latest in luggage and gadgets for making airplanes (and trains, and automobiles) as fun as can be.

Let's face it—traveling, and especially getting out of New York City, can be difficult. Might as well make it fun! Flight 001's New York store resembles a neatly packed suitcase of cutting-edge travel and lifestyle accessories. Whether you are off for the weekend or traveling around the world, you will feel like one of the Avengers as you sweep through the airport terminal in all your retro-future glory. Everything at Flight 001 is designed to look fabulous while making your life utterly convenient. On board, your Salsa Cabin luggage will automatically compress itself to accommodate storage, and pop right back into shape once you land. While in the air, you can stay moisturized and fresh with specially formulated skin care products by Dr. Hauschka. Once you land, you can pop your puppy out of his carrying case and consolidate him, your ID, cell phone, and keys onto an L.A. leash. Flight 001 also has its own line of products, including carrying cases for toiletries, documents, shoes, and more. The store carries Hobo and Jack Spade wallets, Pan Am, Orla Kiely, Tumi luggage and accessories, and more. There are also boutiques in the neighborhood of Cobble Hill in Brooklyn, Los Angeles, San Francisco, and uptown at Henri Bendel's department store. The greatest thing about Flight 001 is that you don't have to be a sucker for design to appreciate the awesome functionality of these products.

Potions, lotions, and pills

Kiehl's (109 Third Avenue, between 13th & 14th Sts., 212-677-3171, Mon–Sat 10–8, Sun 12–6) was renovated and reopened in the East Village last year. A New York institution, Kiehl's continues to innovate in its formulations of luxurious beauty products for the face, body, and hair. Lines include the popular Abyssine line, which uses deep-sea extractions to cure dry skin, and Lycopene line, which uses tomatoes, an excellent antioxidant and natural sun protectant. Even classic items like Kiehl's lip balm are being reinterpreted in new tinted versions. Kiehl's offers three free samples of any other product when you buy something, which is where their in-house philosophy—try before you buy—comes in to great effect. Super-friendly service makes this New York institution well worth a visit.

C.O. Bigelow's Pharmacy, (414 Sixth Avenue, bet. W. 8th and W 9th Sts., 212-793-5433) has been an institution in Greenwich Village for over 150 years, and features an eclectic assortment of toiletries, including scissors, brushes, mirrors, and more, as well as other unrelated feminine necessities, such as beaded evening bags. Bigelow's also offers homeopathic remedies that can be mail-ordered and shipped.

It's difficult to leave **Whole Body** (260 Seventh Avenue at the corner of 25th Street, 212-924-9972, open daily from 9–9) without spending $100. The oils and the organic lotions are exquisite, and they carry the whole Weleda and Burt's Bees lines, and basics like Tom's of Maine toothpaste.

There is always **Sephora** (various locations, check www.sephora.com for details). It's a great place to buy a mini eyeshadow or nail polish for a last-minute date ($3–10). The Sephora brand line of cosmetics are well-formulated and come in a wide spectrum of colors.

Penny's Herb Company (East 7th Street, bet. 1st Avenue and Avenue A, 212-614-0716, by appointment only) is an herbal apothecary and aromatherapy center that does mail order worldwide. Particularly good if you have special health or dietary needs and are looking for an herbal solution rather than a chemical one.

Auto

805 Washington Street, bet. Horatio and Gansevoort Sts.
HOURS: Tu–Sat 12–7; Sun 12–6; closed Mon
Phone: 212-229-2292
WEB: www.thisisauto.com

Auto is a high-end home boutique with a playful sensibility.

You'll find the street Auto is on somewhat quiet, but it's interesting to speculate how this area became popular for stores—it is quite gritty, with old meatpacking factories and real live butchers still working nearby.

Auto presents a refreshingly low-key, worldly, eclectic mix of items for the home, from books to linens to curios. There are downtown brands mixed with high-end items. Unusual, fun, and colorful objects and decorations for the home abound at Auto. The young couple or parent will find much to be excited about here, from absurd objects to Missoni throw pillows and hand towels (from $15). Other items include Eugenia Kim hats ($165–400), hard-to-find local jewelry designers ($50 and up), and paper star lanterns.

The New York Book of Shops

Carry On Tea and Sympathy

✳ 108 Greenwich Avenue, bet. 12th & 13th Sts.

HOURS: Mon–Fri 11–10:30; Sat–Sun 9:30–10:30

PHONE: 212-989-9735

WEB: www.teaandsympathynewyork.com

A typical English restaurant/shop that sells imported British fare and marketplace items for British ex-pats, Anglophiles, and everyone in between.

The restaurant serves such classics as shepherd's pie and, of course, all varieties of ultra-colonial English teas. This will be welcome news to resident British ex-pats, as they are always complaining about how Lipton tastes like dishwater. The shop, which has dark wood-paneled, neatly stocked shelves, feels country-quaint, and sells your favorite British groceries, chocolates, sweets, and teas alongside authentic teapots, mugs, and fun cards. They also carry their own line of T-shirts devoted to the land of the Union Jack. The store does takeout and local deliveries, as well as worldwide shipping of their products. According to this restaurant/shop's website, "carry on tea and sympathy" is an expression that comes from classic English comedy movies.

Tea Leaves

Teany (90 Rivington Street, bet. Ludlow and Orchard Sts., Sun-Thu 10-11; Fri-Sat, 10-1, 212-475-9190) was opened by music superstar Moby and his girlfriend. Both are vegetarian (Moby is a vegan) and the menu features breakfast snacks, salads, and sandwiches, of a vegan bent. Teany has a great afternoon tea special that includes a pot of tea, two of their yummy sandwiches, scone, and petit fours of the day ($16 for one,

$25 for two.) The menu is reasonably priced, and Teany offers a relaxed, unpretentious atmosphere.

Teariffic (51 Mott St. bet. Pell and Bayard Sts., daily 11–11:30, 212-393-9009) is a great little Chinese tapioca tea spot that is a must visit if you make it down to Chinatown. Taro, sesame black tea, and green tea milkshakes rock with or without tapioca.

Up the street, at **Aji Ichiban** (37 Mott Street, daily 10-8:30, 212-233-7650) is a munchies paradise! Meaning "very good" in Japanese, this snack shop stocks bins and bins of all the wasabi peas, jelly candies, and as many snack and candy varieties from across the Pacific as you can stand.

Chance Encounters

Flea markets are not casual outings in New York; they are a way of life. Many New Yorkers hit the flea market every Saturday as a part of their weekend routine. Here is a short guide to some of the best outdoor and indoor flea markets in the city. These markets are particularly good for finding reasonable secondhand clothing, shoes, and accessories.

The Market in Nolita (268 Mulberry Street bet. E. Houston and Prince Sts., open Sat all day). This market features young, up-and-coming, contemporary fashion and accessories designers selling their lines. Worth stopping by if you are looking for something handmade or special.

The Annex (W. 39th St. bet. 9th and 10th Aves., open Sat and Sun).

The Garage Antique Fair and Flea Market (112 W. 25th St. bet. 6th and 7th Aves., Sat and Sun, 6:30–5).

Chelsea Flea Market (29-37 W. 25th St. bet. 5th and 6th Aves., open sunrise to sunset).

These are the three antique and flea markets in the city. Every weekend, rain or shine, dealers from the tri-state (that's New York, New Jersey, and Connecticut) area converge in Chelsea to hawk their wares. Mingle with hipsters and creative types while you browse antique furniture, vintage jeans, furs, costume jewelry, linens, cameras, records, and assorted what have you. Prices are steep by flea standards but be sure to haggle; if you come back at 5 p.m. chances are the dealer will give you a better price to avoid hauling the item back in his truck to wherever he came from. Vintage Rolex Oyster watches start at $1,200, mink coats at about $100. Other Chelsea Flea market staples are African furniture and knickknacks, Tibetan jewelry and art deco lamps. Some vendors will ship internationally.

Williamsburg, Brooklyn

On a sunny Monday afternoon in Williamsburg, people sip iced coffees and meander down Bedford Avenue with a paperback and a dog on leash in tow. The neighborhood feels like an extension of the East Village in Manhattan (a ten-minute subway ride away), and it's become a destination for travelers from all over the world. During the day, Williamsburg effortlessly emulates the Village's easygoing vibe, sparked by the arrival of artists over the past two decades who've introduced a live/work lifestyle to the neighborhood culture. In recent years the neighborhood, especially around the Bedford Ave. subway stop, has developed rapidly to accommodate the many city commuters who have fled Manhattan's escalating rental market. As a result, on weekends Williamsburg bustles just like any neighborhood in Manhattan. It's the kind of place where the day gets away from you while you explore the little shops, galleries, and cafés that line the industrial boulevards, all the way over to the East River. Many shops here are artist-run and eclectic—very laid-back. It has always been a great neighborhood to find excellent vintage, and now showcases the best in hip clothing and furniture design in all of New York.

Jumelle

✳ 148 Bedford Avenue bet. North 8th and 9th Sts.

HOURS: Mon 1–7:30; Tu–Sat 12–7:30; Sun 12–7

PHONE: 718-388-9525

WEB: www.shopjumelle.com

A pioneering, multi-label shop on Williamsburg's main shopping drag.

Candice Waldron brings the same tenacity to running her store as she did to the ten-year journalism career she had prior to opening Jumelle. Open since 2006, the shop has quickly established itself as a welcome addition to the neighborhood. "Before we opened, there was a lot of vintage in Williamsburg, but nothing like what we do," she says. Waldron keeps her ear to the ground by traveling annually to London, Paris, and Scandinavia (a visit to the shop's website will give you the complete rundown, but standouts include Karen Walker, Whyred, HOPE, and hard-to-find shoes by Gaspard Yurkievich). "I'm really big on discovering new designers." Last fall, for instance, she brought British knitwear line Bi La Li stateside. This explains Jumelle's popularity in Williamsburg and beyond—her great taste inspires shoppers' personal styles. "The customers become familiar with the lines, so they come back for them," says Waldron. And, she admits, she's open to tips from visitors. Fitting, as the store attracts tourists from around the world, inspiring Waldron to branch out and usher in even more great new designers.

The Future Perfect

✳ **115 N. 6th Street bet. Berry Street and Wythe Avenue**
HOURS: Daily 12–7
PHONE: 718-599-6278
WEB: www.thefutureperfect.com

A groundbreaking home design store.

The Future Perfect is successful because of its commitment to the best new local and international designers, mostly in the home arena. The store is set up like a museum (you can touch and photograph any of the super-cool objects, sculptures, and other pieces in the store) and the overall feeling is one of a high-craft, high-tech workshop where everything is both functional and beautiful. Even the cash-wrap looks like something stolen from a deep forest hideout—intricately woven

pieces of plywood that cleverly accommodate traditional desk items. Downstairs, a small gallery exhibits art reflecting FP's sustainable, "future-conscious" aesthetic. Highlights in the store are intricate but modern wood screens ($1,800); a toile sofa with "revisionist" embroidery ($3,000); a variety of fantastical chandeliers ($700–5,000); a coffee table fashioned from the deck and wheels of a skateboard; as well as tons of fascinating objects like mouth-blown decanters ($500), glass skulls ($200), and plastic vases ($12). Key designers in the store include Jason Miller, Scrapile, Esque, Qubus, DFC, and Timorous Beasties wallpaper. Don't worry if you haven't heard of them . . . you will soon!

Furniture and Home Shopping in Williamsburg

Williamsburg has some great out-of-the-way spots to get new and used furniture. Just ask a local on Bedford Avenue to point you in the direction of the water, if you can't see it already . . .

Two Jakes Used Office Furniture (320 Wythe Ave., bet. Grand and S. 1st Sts., 718-782-7780, www. twojakes.com). If you've ever thought to refinish an old piece of furniture but haven't, the Two Jakes have made your procrastination their livelihood. The store collects old-school metal and wood office desks, chairs, and tables, and refinishes them in a modern way. Stripped, minimal, and clean, if you didn't like vintage furniture because it was too baroque, they've solved the problem for you. A bit on the pricey side but worth it if you can find the perfect piece for your office. They also accept donations; call for more information.

Moon River Chattel (62 Grand Street, bet. Wythe and Kent Aves, www.moonriverchattel.com, 718-388-1121) is a poetically named little shop that seems as though it should be in the Berkshires, but is tucked away on Grand Street near the waterfront, it's a hidden treasure. Moon River carries refurbished home furnishings and old-fashioned housewares: linens, dishes, kitchen items, tin toys, and an assortment of old-fashioned books. Many items are reproductions of rare objects found in the '40s and '50s, but some are originals. On your way out, treat yourself to a piece of penny candy from the selection on the counter, or purchase a soda pop from an old-time fridge, the kind that June Cleaver called an "icebox."

Catbird

❋ 390 Metropolitan Avenue bet. Marcy and Havemeyer
HOURS: Mon–Fri 1–8; Sat–Sun 12–8
PHONE: 718-388-7688
WEBSITE: www.catbirdnyc.com
219 Bedford Avenue bet. North 4th and 5th Sts.
HOURS: Mon–Fri 1–8; Sat–Sun 12–8
PHONE: 718-599-3457

Jewel-box–sized space offers the crème de la crème in local jewelry design, plus clothing and accessories.

"I live in Williamsburg on the south side and there was basically nowhere to shop, so I opened Catbird," says owner

Rony Vardi. Now in its third year, she has expanded from Location 1 (on Metropolitan) to focus on her rarefied collection of local and hard-to-find jewelry designers at Location 2 (on Bedford).

At the Metropolitan location, you will find complementary clothing and shoes at a wide range of prices, as well as what Vardi claims is "the best denim selection in Williamsburg, hands down." She carries hard-to-find brands like Deener, Jordache, Odyn, and Aoki as well as better-known ones like J Brand and Wrangler (all $69–220). This location also features stationery from local designers like Jezebel, a playfully artistic paper line that mixes nineteenth-century silhouettes with twenty-first-century epigraphs.

Closer to the action on Bedford, Catbird's second location grew organically from Vardi's relationships with New York's coolest jewelry designers (hooray for all the smart, crafty people in the world!). The store is known for its well-edited selection and is a great place to find unusual pieces such as delicate, chain-link rings ($60); charms from Oath NYC, modeled after things one would find at the bottom of a purse ($280); handmade silk ribbons à la *Best in Show* ($6–8); pirate and astronaut pendants from Vera Meat ($140–240); and tongue-in-cheek 18th-century references in pieces from Bittersweets New York (around $295; shop at 37 Broadway bet. Wythe and Kent, Wed–Sun 3–8, 718-218-8595); and other pieces from the store's own collection. This store also carries John Derian glassware ($40–200; see **John Derian Co.** boutique, p. 9). Everything about Catbird quietly affirms great taste, all the way to the edges of the vintage French wallpaper. Gift certificates are also available.

Paper Shops

Great paper makes a bold statement, as many busy New Yorkers will testify. Whether you are buying a gift, putting together a job application, or dropping someone an enticing note, here are an assortment of some paper shops around the city where you are likely to find high quality, unique stationery, notebooks, and pens.

Greenwich Letterpress (39 Christopher Street bet. Waverly Pl. and Seventh Ave., 212-989-7464, Mon 1–6, Tu–Fri 11–7, Sat–Sun 12–6, www.greenwichletterpress. com). A Greenwich Village-style education in the art of paper, this shop prides itself on utilizing older paper- and stationery-making techniques (see the website for their fascinating story.) The store's line mixes contemporary styling with old-fashioned letterpress quality. GL carries limited-edition artist-designed collections, and a wide array of cards and paper by some of the best small presses in the country. Custom letterpress is available by appointment.

JAM Paper and Envelope (135 3rd Ave., bet. E. 14th and E. 15th Sts., 212-473-6666, Mon–Fri 8:30–7, Sat and Sun 10–6, www.jampaper.com) stocks paper in brightly colored hues more traditional stationery stores shy away from. They also print business cards cheaply on bright (or not) colored card stock. Also at: 611 Sixth Ave., at W. 18th Street, 212-255-4593; check the website for additional address information.

Kate's Paperie (561 Broadway bet. Prince and Spring Sts., 212-941-9816, Mon–Sat 10–8, Sun 11–7, www.katespaperie.com). This is probably the most popular (and populist) place in the city to find stationery and other paper products, including fancy gift wrap, ribbon, bags and boxes, planners, invitations, photo frames, albums, and all kinds of other containing, framing, organizing, and fun stuff. Kate's carries indulgent paper bonds and stocks, as well as luxury items for the study, credenzas, and fancy letter openers and the like. They stock an excellent selection of pens as well. Check the website for an online store.

Pearl Paint (308 Canal Street, bet. Broadway and Mercer St., 212-431-7932, Mon–Fri 9–7, Sat 10–6:30, Sun 10–6, www.pearlpaint.com) is the mother of all art stores in the city, and you can find virtually any framing, storage or archival material here, as well as a range of papers, paints, pens, albums, tools, and more. The store is five floors of anything you could possibly need to fulfill any creative urge, and prices are reasonable. Check the website for details.

Paper Presentation (23 W. 18th Street, bet. 5th and 6th Aves., 212-463-7035, Mon 9–7, Tu–Thu 9–8, Fri 9–7, Sat 11–6, Sun 12–6, www.paperpresentation.com). This spacious store, just north of Union Square, stocks materials for archiving letters and photos, stationery, picture frames, and unusual greeting cards.

Cat Fish Greetings Inc. (219A Mulberry Street, bet. Spring and Broome Sts., 212-625-1800, Mon–Sat, 10:30–8, Sun 12–6, www.catfishgreetings.com) specializes in greeting card and invitation designs created using special textured paper. The store has a catalog of the simple, contemporary designs on offer. The combination of ink-on-paper with a three-dimensional blending of fine papers and objects make the cards tactile and fun. There are different lines of cards to choose from in colorful papers, themes, and characters. Cat Fish also sells great Japanese and technology-inspired gifts like desk accessories, CD cases, albums, and more. Prices for stationery run about $10 and up; greeting cards are $5.

You got the write stuff, baby

Some people love cars. Others, shoes. And some of us, pens. Going to write something? Gotta have a great pen. Here are three renowned pen stores in Manhattan, in order from oldest to youngest, where you will find the pen of your dreams.

Fountain Pen Hospital (10 Warren Street, bet. Broadway and Church Sts., Mon–Fri 7:45–5:45, Sat–Sun 9–5:30, 212-964-0580, www.fountainpenhospital.com). The store was founded in 1946, and this family business continues to be the granddaddy of writing implements in the city. Did you know there was a magazine called *Pen World* or *The Pennant*? Me neither, but if you know someone who loves pens, they might be delighted to hear that the owner is a regular contributor to these publications. Seriously, find any pen your heart desires here. Special and custom orders available—just visit the store.

Joon (Grand Central Terminal, Lexington Ave & 42nd Street, Mon–Fri 8–8, Sat 10–6, Sun 12–5, 212-949-1702, www.joonpens.com) is another of these New York pen institutions. They carry your Parker, your Mont Blanc, your Fisher, your Cartier . . . need I say more? Located inside Grand Central, this is a good excuse for you to visit one of the most beautiful buildings in New York, and then write to your mom about it.

Berliner Pen (928 Broadway bet. 21st and 22nd Sts., Suite 203, Mon–Fri 10–1, 212-614-3020). Berliner

Pen sells both vintage and contemporary writing instruments. They also provide services such as repairing older, hard-to-service pens, and museum-quality restoration services to antique pens. It's heartening to think about pens being preserved as the artifacts they are quickly becoming.

Sodafine

❋ 119 Grand Street, bet. Berry and Wythe Aves.
HOURS: Tues–Sat 12–7; Sun 1–6
PHONE: 718-230-3060
WEB: www.sodafine.com

Sodafine is a pioneering artist-run boutique specializing in DIY, craft, and eco-friendly clothing, accessories, and gifts.

Sodafine originally opened in Philadelphia and moved to New York to join a larger community of artists-cum-fashion designers and vintage connoisseurs. Since its Brooklyn opening in 2003, Sodafine has manifested a crafty, DIY sensibility that resonated enough in Fort Greene, Brooklyn, for owner Erin Weckerle to expand operations to the more retail-centric Williamsburg area. Sodafine is funky, colorful, diverse, and laid-back, and the merchandise inspires the imagination. The shapes of the clothes and handbags are amorphous and unconventional—hems and seams are not where they should be, and this off-kilter approach to fashion is what Sodafine is all about. However, most pieces in the store can be mixed and incorporated into a contemporary wardrobe. Weckerle designs her own line of hand-knit and crocheted earrings, sweaters, hats, and scarves called Purldrop. She also carries gift items like stationery, calendars, bath products, and candles by designers like Little Otsu, Nikki McClure, Slingshot!, SweetThunder, Three Sisters, and others. She's expanded Sodafine's inventory to include more lines that utilize eco-friendly principles and sustainable labor practices, such as Passenger Pigeon; Popomomo (handmade, one-of-a-kind), Organic by John Patrick; Melissa shoes (rubber shoes from Brazil); Bahar Shahpar and Valhalla, both Brooklyn-based; and Loyale, another New York-based eco-line. Vintage merchandise rounds out the handmade designs in the store. "Vintage has the same unique, one-of-a-kind feeling that our handmade items have," Erin explains. "We want to provide an interesting model of the intersection of art, craft, and fashion at work in everyday life."

Trimmings, trinkets, and more

Perhaps you have an earring that's missing a bead, or you've picked up a fabulous choker missing a rhinestone at the Chelsea Flea Market (p.64) last weekend. There are plenty of places you can visit to have your jewelry added onto or fixed.

Toho Shoji (990 Ave. of the Americas, bet. W. 36th and W. 37th Sts., Mon–Fri 9–7, Sat 10–6, Sun 10–5, 212-868-7466, www.tohoshoji-ny.com). This longstanding jewelry components store has been in the garment district for over twenty years. Toho Shoji sells plating, ornaments, binding, beads, silver chains, and much more, individually or wholesale.

Beads of Paradise, (16 E. 17th Street, bet. Broadway and 5th Ave., Daily 11–7:30, 212-620-0642). Mosey over to this bead emporium to have any jewelry finds altered or fixed. You can find beads and crafts from other countries as well. There are vials of colored beads

($3.50) everywhere in this tiny, brightly colored shop, and for the superstitious, notes on which stones will bring power, love, or luck. If you don't know what to do with the myriad of objects, sign up for a weekend crash course in jewelry making ($55–$75).

Artistic Ribbon, Inc. (22 W. 21st Street, bet. 5th and 6th Aves., Mon–Fri 8–4, 212-255-4224, www. artisticribbon.com). Artistic Ribbon sells every kind of ribbon imaginable—solids, stripes, dots, jacquard, silk, satin, etc.—at wholesale prices only, which makes it very cheap ($7–10 for 100 yards of most varieties.) Visit their website or their office for a catalog. Another great ribbon shop is **So-Good** (28 W. 38th St., bet 5th and 6th Aves., 212-398-0236, Mon–Fri 9–5), where you can buy beautiful grosgrain, and other ribbon at any length for a very reasonable price.

Mini Mini Market

※ 218 Bedford Ave., corner of N. 5th Street
HOURS: Mon–Fri 12–9; Sat–Sun 12–8
PHONE: 718-302-9337
WEB: miniminimarket.com

1980s pop memorabilia and candy-colorful clothing and accessories fill this fun shop, modeled after a neighborhood corner store.

Growing up, my sister's bedroom was as pink as a pill. Her dresser was a tall white chest with carved legs, and gold-painted detail. An illustrated portrait of a pre-anime child hung on the wall. I spent hours in my sister's bedroom, reading books and magazines, eating candy, playing games, dressing up, and losing track of time. Mini Mini Market captures the essence of these hours by stocking the memorabilia of my childhood with the impeccable aplomb of a Wes Anderson film. Dana May Schwister and Erika Louise Vala modeled Mini Mini Market after a corner store, where one could pick up anything from a birthday card to a candy bar to a small gift. They stock the store's walls and shelves with "things we loved from when we were ten, in the early '80s." The shop is a *Valley of the Dolls* costume closet for Williamsburg girls.

Mini Mini carries local designers, as well as some from Japan; dresses range reasonably from $58–110, with the occasional $200 piece. There is something to behold in every part of the recently remodeled store, including toys, visors, flip flops, sunglasses, parasols, sundresses, T-shirts, stickers (yes, the kind you collected), dolls, pillows, dishes, jewelry, albums, and stationery. The store also carries a small selection of shoes ($30–100). (Also, check out the newest addition to the Mini Mini universe: Shoe Market, 160 N. 9th Street at Bedford Ave., 718-388-8495.) Most smaller gift items are between $2–20; clothing ranges from $15–200; shoes go from $40–100; and jewelry costs around $30.

Fluke

❈ 169 Wythe Avenue between N. 5th and N. 6th Sts.
HOURS: Wed–Thu 1–7:30; Fri 2:30–7:30; Sat 1–7:30, Sun 12:30–7; closed Mon–Tu
PHONE: 718-486-3166

A veteran vintage shop that holds court in bright, airy Williamsburg digs.

Despite its name, it's no coincidence that Fluke is a success. The shop feels special the moment you walk in—it has a nostalgic air, and is filled with clothing and accessories that pique the imagination. After a brief stint in film and a couple of other odd jobs, Castleman set up shop in 2002 (another era in Williamsburg), "behind a falafel shop on Bedford. You had to walk down a hall, past a psychic to get to my shop."

Today, gone-but-not-forgotten rockabilly tunes waft through the new large, airy space, which is anchored at center by an inviting chaise lounge and a collection of rare issues of *Playboy*, *Esquire*, and other seminal style publications, augmenting the atmosphere of worlds gone by. The West Coast native shops all over the country for high-quality vintage, and doesn't discriminate against non-designer labels like other stores in the city. "I look for interesting things, and if I find a good designer, then all the better." Prices start at $30 and average around $50–75. Shoes average $50–60. Though you could get lost in its timeless feeling of dusty Americana, Fluke happens to be located at the apex of a hip hangout hub between N. 6th and N. 7th Sts. (performance and art space **Galapagos** is on N. 6th, while the restaurant/screening room **Monkeytown** is nearby on N. 7th).

Lower East Side

Most walking tours of the Lower East Side will meet in front of the infamous Katz's Deli (205 E. Houston Street at the corner of Ludlow Street, 212-254-2246). Katz's is an institution that's seen the scene move from hard to hip in the last ten years; the restaurant has hosted meetings of gangsters, as well as the famous orgasm scene in *When Harry Met Sally*. Today, the Lower East Side is filled with hip boutiques, restaurants, and cafés, but the gritty character remains. Some new businesses have tried to assimilate to the neighborhood by leaving storefronts intact—others, like the gargantuan Hotel on Rivington, have not. Street art and old school businesses are still plentiful, especially further east. The Lower East Side remains a vibrant cultural center for young New Yorkers as well as the Latin community. Hungry? If you walk east to Clinton Street, you will find some of the best dining in the city.

Honey in the Rough

✳ 161 Rivington Street bet. Suffolk and Clinton Sts.

HOURS: Mon–Sat 12–8; Sun 12–7

PHONE: 212-228-6415

WEB: www.honeyintherough.com

Your "dream dress" closet.

If you love wearing super-interesting, one-of-only-a-few dresses and feeling like a million bucks when you shop, the one store you must visit on the Lower East Side is Honey in the Rough. Owner Ashley Hanosh, in addition to being one of the nicest NYC proprietors you'll meet, carries an unparalleled selection of dresses and jewelry from all over the world. Hanosh aims to serve any and every type of customer who walks in the store by stocking designers with different points of view. "I'm definitely not trying to exclude anyone," she says cheerfully, and lucky for us. Tsumori Chisato produces exquisite dresses ($550–1,500) that have earned her the nickname "the Zac Posen of Japan," according to Hanosh, primarily because of Chisato's innovative techniques, like painting on velvet. Other lines include Sue Stemp; Antipodium, a hard-to-find British line; local designer Mociun, whose versatile dresses ($300–480) are constructed from hand-printed fabric, making them an HOTR staple; Alice McCall, an Aussie designer with her own unique take on the cocktail dress ($400–600); NYC cult designer Judi Rosen ($300–500); and Samantha Pleet ($290–460). Hanosh also stocks more mainstream brands for the celebrity-style-conscious gal, like Thread Social ($600–800) and Madison Marcus ($255–400). Nevertheless, Hanosh definitely has her own taste: "I'm all about detail, texture, fabrics, and buttons." As if all these beautiful dresses weren't enough, Hanosh also brandishes her knowledge of jewelry craft and design (both her parents are jewelry designers) with the baubles in the store. She features up-and-comers like Sabrina Dinoff, and the innovative Losselliani, who produces spectacular museum-quality jewelry, ranging in price from $200–1,500, depending on the materials. Go there now! Also, come by the store on a Saturday to experience the work of "the most amazing eyebrow sculptor." A fitting way to get ready for that party you'll be wearing your new dress to.

Bblessing

The New York Book of Shops

❊ 181 Orchard Street bet. Stanton and Houston Sts.

HOURS: Mon–Sat 1–9; Sun 12–8

PHONE: 212-378-8005

WEBSITE: www.bblessing.com

A trendsetting men's lifestyle boutique featuring impeccable interiors.

The mission at Bblessing is to turn your idea of men's shopping upside down. A spokesperson for the store says that Bblessing is dedicated to "the bleeding edge in men's fashion, art, music, literature, and film in a constantly changing atmosphere." And what an atmosphere it is. By using traditional furniture as avant-garde design touches, co-owner Daniel Jackson has lovingly created an impressive interior—a capsized table is suspended from the ceiling and functions as a clothing rack; upside-down desk lamps line the ceiling in a mesmerizing parade; and a chandelier fashioned from glass paraphernalia (*very* downtown) hangs in the midst of it all. You'll feel satisfied just having visited, but don't stop there. Bblessing is known for its pitch-perfect selection of men's streetwear brands, including Rag & Bone, Preen, Raf Simons, Patrick Ervell, Giacometti, Surface To Air, and Bblessing (the house label). The store also showcases limited-edition accessories and artwork by local designers. A true hidden gem at Bblessing is a secret doorway in back that leads to what used to be Breakbeat Science, a music store specializing in vinyl records where massive speakers hang from the ceiling. The store frequently hosts openings for artists, which you can find out about on their website. Blessed, indeed.

Exceptional Tailors

A great tailor can be a magician; a Salvation Army suit can be transformed into Brit pop glamour. The White House has called upon the services of the same tailor for many years, and England's Savile Row is world-famous. How can you (and your wardrobe) enjoy the same loving care? Read on: from buttoned-up to Bohemian, New York's tailors cater to a broad range of tastes and styles with low- to high-end custom services.

Ignacio Tailor (119 E. 60th Street, 2nd floor, bet. Park and Lexington Aves., 212-758-2747, Mon–Fri 9–7, Sat 9–3). All of the designer flagship stores on upper Madison Avenue send their customers to Ignacio for his excellent alterations, particularly for pants—either resizing or taking up. Pant hems average $15, and altering a dress or jacket starts at around $40.

New York is probably the only city where you can find full businesses operating in extremely small spaces, especially all over the Lower East Side, Chinatown, and Nolita. **Victor and Jose Tailor** (205 Mott Street, bet. Spring and Broome Sts., 212-941-0348, Mon–Sat 11–8), whip up a solid pant hem for $5. That's right—no more and no less. Something complicated, like altering a fully beaded top, will cost you about half of what an uptown tailor would charge ($30).

À la bazaar tailors in Hong Kong, India, and Morocco, there are New York tailors who will duplicate designer suits. Give them the suit you like, and the fabric, and they will copy it stitch for stitch, made to measure. **LNK Custom Tailoring** (178 Mulberry Street, bet. Broome and Kenmare Sts., 212-226-7755, Mon–Sat 11–8, Sun by appointment), will make you any suit you like for $700. If you add in the value of his being at your disposal, you might just get more than you bargained for.

Marrakech Tailor (76 E. 7th Street bet. 1st and 2nd Aves., 212-780-9574, Mon–Sat 9:30–6, www .marrakechtailors.com), is my personal go-to for more complicated alterations of any kind, including re-shaping a dress entirely. The owner will work patiently with you until it's just right. An average alteration costs $20.

Le Sous Sol

❊ 137 Rivington Street bet. Suffolk and Norfolk Sts.
(lower east level)
HOURS: Daily 12–8
TELEPHONE: 212-477-7723
WEBSITE: www.lesoussol.com

A NYC bastion of Antwerp fashion design.

This outlet for the fashion-design-obsessed opened in late 2007 and is truly one of a kind. The proprietors, Sarah B. Yormick and her sister Linda Belkebir, bring an extra-special European touch to their mission: to showcase the best minimal design from the burgeoning fashion center of Antwerp, Belgium. This store isn't for the faint of heart, in a fashion or financial sense (clothing runs between around $200 and $2,500), but Yormick says that she and Belkebir are meeting a demand, a relief for anyone who fears New York may no longer be a fashion epicenter. Standouts include Jean Paul Knott, a former Yves Saint Laurent designer whose satin trousers held up by delicate spaghetti suspender straps are theatrical and inspiring; Jessie Lecomte, whose pieces are hand painted by a Belgian artist; AF Vandervorst, a comparatively well-known former Jean Paul Gaultier designer;

paneled knits from Caroline Foulon; and bags by two designers, Sophie D'Hoore and Eric Beaudin (D'Hoore's large carry-ons are made from vintage recycled motorcycle jackets). The space is a beautifully conceived ode to the darker aesthetics of its sartorial occupants, and will surely inspire every visitor to peruse the stack of books the store keeps on hand to educate patrons further about influential Antwerp fashion designers.

Dear:55

❖ 55 Clinton Street bet. Stanton and Rivington Sts.
HOURS: Daily 1–9
PHONE: 212-673-3494

International vintage and craft fill this white-walled LES boutique.

Clinton Street maintains a discreet charm in a neighborhood where longtime local businesses thrive alongside newer ones. It is here you will stumble across an unusual alabaster Tim Burton-esque setting. A white bench, a white bicycle, and a whimsical window installation that serve as the opening montage to Dear:55's modern, wall-to-wall white space. Wander inside to find a large birdcage housing jewelry handmade from found objects by one of the store's co-owners, Hey Ja Do. A look along the walls reveals a wide selection of urban and Zen-inspired vintage carefully selected from fashion capitals like Japan and Paris. Highlights include '80s pieces from Yohji Yamamoto and Rei Kawakubo of Commes des Garçons, as well as new collections from an eclectic mix of Japanese and European designers. Despite this international flair, both the store and the merchandise evoke a 1970s and '80s New York sensibility—think *Liquid Sky*, Jean-Michel Basquiat, and

Studio 54—of downtown artists crafting not only their work, but also their clothing. "It's great over here on Clinton Street because it still feels like the old New York, when small boutiques were everywhere," says the store's other co-owner, Moon Rhee. Participate in Dear:55's celebration of the near-extinct independent downtown boutique with some DIY-inspired revelry of your own.

Project No. 8

✳ 138 Division Street bet. Ludlow and Canal Sts.
HOURS: Tu–Wed, Sun 1–8; Thu–Sat 1–9; closed Mon
PHONE: 212-925-5599
WEB: www.projectno8.com

*Chinatown shop specializing in hard-to-find
fashion and worship-worthy designer objects.*

For some minimal glamour that's New York by way of Berlin, London, Japan, and beyond, head south to Project No. 8. This shop is the eighth installment of an ongoing collaboration between Berlin-based owners Brian Janusiak and Elizabeth Beer called Various Projects. Janusiak, a professor of graphic design, works in both the art and design arenas in a "project-based manner." Beer is a clothing designer and gallerist, and the two joined forces in 2005 to explore a multidisciplinary design partnership. "Having a retail space is a chance for us to experiment—more publicly—with some themes that recur in our own work," says Janusiak. Project No. 8's uber design-conscious aesthetic begins with the ground beneath your feet. The floor is a "sustainable-building" sun study (an examination of the kind of light that enters the store throughout the year) conducted by the store's architect. The store also boasts a vacuum-sealed storefront in combination with a radiant floor for heating the space. Objects and clothing receive no lesser degree of tender loving care. Find excellent, highly wearable looks from international fashion vanguards (London's Boudicca and the peerless Parisian Martin Margiela) to excellent local designers, such as Sunshine and Shadow and A Détacher.

Best of all, you are likely to come across someone and something you've never heard of before, for instance, a black canvas tote by a local product designer with a long, pull-out chute lined with a dozen pockets. Don't pass by the accessories case, which is filled with a rotating cast of super sexy objects, like smooth, beige, calfskin mittens from Margiela ($285); delicate, soft, screen-printed driving gloves from Boudicca ($185); a men's Italian snake "stingray" wallet ($210); and a smooth black cuff of vintage animal horn, contemporized by the artist Chris Bundy ($695). Janusiak and Beer travel frequently and regularly introduce clothing, accessories, and an assortment of objects made by talented artists and designers worldwide. "We imagine the store to be in part a place for the projects these artists have no immediate or obvious home for," says Janusiak. To find out more from the fascinating minds of Various Projects, be sure to stop in and say hello to Lydia, the store's manager (who keeps more merchandise in the back of the store, so don't hesitate to ask).

Casa de Rodriguez

❊ 156 Stanton Street, bet. Suffolk and Clinton Sts.

HOURS: Daily 12–7

PHONE: 212-995-8880

WEB: www.casaderodriguez.com

Jody and David Rodriguez make beautiful, highly wearable, fashion-forward hats.

In the past, Casa de Rodriguez has retailed at major department stores like Barney's, but the neighborhood is lucky to have this little Lower East Side boutique. "We've always been a little ahead of our time," Jody told me. "That's what it takes when you are wearing hats—you are on the forefront of fashion." Indeed, each hat in the shop could transform not only one's appearance, but outlook. The oversized berets evoke an ultra-mod French girl on the back of a Vespa. The fur newsboy hats are cute and practical, for New York winter shopping excursions. The details in the lining and embellishments are what make these hats stand out—the rings fabricated from different materials, the soft suede bands around the brims, and the unique fabrics.

"You can come in and buy a hat and put it in the closet for a couple of years, and then take it out and feel very confident about wearing it," Jody says. Each hat has a classic shape, but with a modern twist that makes it fun. Casa de Rodriguez also does custom hat design and fittings—just ask. Hats range in price from $75–750.

Hats

Yes, it's true, hats are for trendsetters, and here's a list of hat shops that will get your head in the right place for any season or reason.

The Village Scandal (19 E. 7th Street, bet. 2nd Ave. and Cooper Square, 212-460-9358, Mon–Sat 12 noon–12 midnight, Sun 1–11, www.villagescandal.com). Retro hats are the look here. Milliners like the San Francisco Hat Company lend a snazzy collection of newsboy, fedora, and other assorted classic hat shapes, in different fabrications (tweed, leather, fur, silk, etc.) to the mix. The proof is in the details—real ostrich feathers, crocodile trim, and lace. Handbags and other accessories (brooches, earrings, necklaces, and more) are also worth a peek. Open until midnight most days, for those last minute fashion turnabouts. Hats run between $25–500.

Lisa Shaub (232 Mulberry Street, 212-965-9176, Wed 12–5, Thu 12–7, Fri 4–7, Sat 12–7, Sun 1–6, www.lisashaub.com). Lisa Shaub makes jewel-toned, 1920s and '30s-inspired fedoras, cloches, berets, and more, in felt, velvet, and other opulent fabrics that mold to your head and your personality. Her hats can't be beat for making you look more glamorous than you do in your recurring dream where you're moonlighting as a nightclub singer, à la Billie Holliday. Shaub also does custom work. Her hats start at around $150 each, and she also sells evening bags, scarves, sarongs, straw beach bags, and feather headpieces.

Edith Machinist

❉ 104 Rivington Street, bet. Essex and Ludlow Sts.

HOURS: Mon–Fri 1–8; Sat–Sun 12–8

PHONE: 212-979-9992

A shopper's paradise/warehouse of hundreds of well-edited vintage women's clothing and shoes.

The windows at this basement-level shop tickle the fashion itch—usually an amazing dress, bag, and pair of shoes are irresistibly on display. Edith Machinist is the mecca for vintage shoes and handbags from every era. Open for six years, the shop's popularity has spread almost strictly through word of mouth, from here to Tokyo. Find vintage for any occasion here—whether it's going to a rodeo, taking a drive through the country, or attending the Costume Gala at the Metropolitan Museum of Art. Edith Machinist has created a permanent indoor flea market, with merchandise spilling off the racks and shoes lining the floor like they are going out of style—which technically, they once did, but who's cashing in now?

"We are interested in finding things that have style on their own, versus buying strictly designers," Machinist told me. However, there are still plenty of vintage Armani dresses, YSL blazers, and Gucci purses to die for. Next time you are looking for something unusual to offset your jeans, look no further than the gems Edith's dug up for you. Prices range from $25 and up.

Sweet Candy

The sweet tooth usually rears its head when you're on a shopping high, and there are several spots on the Lower East Side that will feed the beast. In fact, these are some of the premier sweet spots in Manhattan, and part of the reason the neighborhood is more of a destination than ever.

When you're done picking a rainbow of handbags and shoes at Edith Machinist, stop by **Economy Candy** (108 Rivington Street bet. Ludlow and Essex Sts., Sun–Fri 9–6, Sat 10–5, 212-254-1531) next door and get your sugar fix from any variety of candy ever made. The store has been a neighborhood fixture for over thirty years. You can find gummy anything-your-heart-desires, a wide variety of international chocolates and caramels, kitschy wrapped candies (crazy, popping, or blue, it's all here!) and treats from your childhood, as well as a variety of other sweets, teas, and sundries.

Just up the street is the **Sugar Sweet Sunshine Bakery** (126 Rivington Street bet. Essex and Norfolk Sts., Mon–Thu 8–10, Fri 8–11, Sat 10–11, Sun 10–7, 212-995-1960), where the atmosphere is as relaxed as the air is sweet. Cupcakes are the specialty, and the two always-present bakers take suggestions from customers seeking the recipes they grew up with. Look for red velvet with satin vanilla butter cream, pumpkin (instead of carrot cake) with cream cheese icing, lemon with lemon butter cream, yellow cake with almond butter cream (called "Bob" because it's all American), and chocolate on chocolate (called "Ooey-gooey"). They also bake cakes to order and feature other sweets, like mini-cheesecakes and brownies.

Il Laboratorio del Gelato (95 Orchard Street, Daily 10–6, 212-343-9922). Opened by Jon Snyder, the founder and creator of the popular gelato brand Ciao Bella, this shop is located across the street from the **Lower East Side Tenement Museum** (p. 93), and next door to one of two rival pickle stands. The space resembles a spotless, ultra-chic lab (hence the name) with staff in white coats, busy perfecting a batch of gelato. A small freezer up front advertises the twelve flavors of the day. Flavors are rotated daily, so each day brings something new. In all, there are at least seventy-five flavors available, including cinnamon, coconut, papaya, and more standard flavors (well, sometimes). Doors close promptly at 6 p.m., so a visit is the perfect ending to a weekday afternoon of shopping.

A bit further north in the East Village, **ChikaLicious** (203 E. 10th Street bet. 1st and 2nd Aves., Wed–Sun 3–11:30, no reservations, 212-995-9511), is an infamous dessert-only restaurant, featuring a sushi-style, a la carte dessert bar. Offerings include a three-course prix fixe menu, consisting of an "amuse" (appetizer), entree, dessert, and assorted petit fours for $12—add $7 for wine pairings.

Doyle & Doyle

❖ 189 Orchard Street, bet. E. Houston and Stanton Sts.

HOURS: Tu–Sun 1–7; Thu 1–8; closed Mon

PHONE: 212-677-9991

WEB: www.doyledoyle.com

Get an education in fine estate and antique jewelry.

Want to learn more about jewelry bought from estates and antique collections? A visit to Doyle and Doyle could certainly be your crash course. Here, the jewelry sells in the tens of thousands. The jewelry is ethereal and otherworldly. Sisters Pam and Elizabeth Doyle are both trained gemologists, who opened the shop in 2000, showcasing an inventory of antique and vintage pieces handpicked from estates. The Doyle & Doyle estate and antique jewelry collection includes pieces from the Georgian, Victorian, Edwardian, Art Nouveau, Art Deco, and Retro periods. Their contemporary private label collection reflects these sensibilities. The Doyles think about color and its relationship to emotion in their design, as well as the historical meaning certain shapes, stones, and designs. If you are looking for something extra special, the jewelry here is to die for.

Jewelry Repair

These are a couple of spots in Manhattan highly recommended for jewelry repair, especially trickier jobs:

Silver World (126 Macdougal Street, bet. West 3rd and Bleecker Sts., 212-353-8747, Mon–Fri 1–9, Sat–Sun 1–11). An old school jewelry repair store in Soho where simple mistakes are fixed on the premises, and more complicated ones are tenderly resolved within a fortnight.

Metalliferous (34 W. 46th Street, bet. 5th and 6th Aves., 212-944-0909, Mon–Fri 8:30–6, Sat 10–3, www.metalliferous.com). Metalliferous is a full-service, fully stocked supplier of metal, tools, and supplies to jewelers, crafters, hobbyists, metalworkers, sculptors, and everyone else interested in metalworking and jewelry. The store features classic antique tools, discounted and used jewelry parts, and other rare finds. So if you want to add a lightning bolt charm to that Tiffany bracelet . . . bring 'er here.

Miks

❊ 100 Stanton Street, bet. Orchard and Ludlow Sts.
HOURS: Tu–Sun 1–8; closed Mon
PHONE: 212-505-1982

Find a playful twist on everyday basics and streetwear—and a great reason to never shop at American Apparel again.

Mitsuyo Toyota, the designer at Miks, utilizes mod shapes and graphic design to inform her casual clothing collection. The collection consists of staple tops and bottoms with twists on the shapes, seams, colors, and details. In particular, if you are seeking an alternative to casual clothing, Toyota does a great job of making well-designed, affordable separates, like a striped tank top, a shawl-collar sweatshirt, and great T-shirts. Miks's appeal lies in its universality—you are just as likely to find a hip kid shopping in here as someone a bit more conservative who's looking for a wardrobe face-lift. If Old Navy commercials and "office casual" are driving you up the wall, pay Miks a visit.

Tops are $80; sweaters range up to $160; skirts and pants are $130; limited edition Converse sneakers are $88; and coats and jackets are $280.

Galleries etc. on the Lower East Side

LES galleries feature newer, up-and-coming artists, and are worth swinging by if you're up for a little diversion from shopping. What's cool about these spaces is the surrounding environment. Often, gallery hopping in Chelsea, New York's current art hub, can be daunting and unpleasant, mostly because Chelsea is located in a far western reach of Manhattan. Popping into a gallery is much more manageable here.

Rivington Arms (4 E. 2nd St. bet. Bowery and 2nd Ave., 1st fl., 646-654-3213, Wed–Fri 11–6; Sat–Sun 12–6, also by appointment, www.rivingtonarms.com). The gallery features photography, painting, and installations that range in scope from politics to popular culture. At the **Reed Space**, (151 Orchard Street bet. Rivington and Stanton Sts., 212-253-0588, Daily 1–7, www.thereedspace.com), which is actually more of a store than a gallery, you can find the latest in media, technology, graphic design, and fashion streetwear. Opened by

Staple Design, the idea is to display the intersection between communications, art, and pop culture. There are some limited edition books, sneakers, and toys here. The cutely named **Cuchifritos** is the gallery arm of the Artists Alliance Inc., a downtown art initiative devoted to public space, community, and social issues. Cuchifritos is located inside the Essex Street Market (120 Essex Street, bet. Delancey and Rivington Sts.), at the southern end of the building. **The Essex Street Market**, by the way, is a great place to pick up an inexpensive snack or a fresh juice (fruit or vegetable). Lastly, there is the **Lower East Side Tenement Museum** (97 Orchard Street bet. Broome and Delancey Sts., Visitor's Center Hours: Mon–Fri 11–5:30, Sat–Sun 10:45–5:30). The building is available for viewing via guided tour only. For more information, visit the web site at www. tenement.org. It's neat to walk through the streets and catch glimpses of the ghosts of people past in the fresh face of one of New York City's most historically rich neighborhoods.

For a snack, check out **Brown** (61 Hester Street, bet. Grand and Canal Sts., 212-254-9825, $5.50–$9.50 for lunch items). Located a few blocks from the Lower East Side Tenement Museum, the menu features a variety of organic sandwiches, salads, and soups. Also great for sipping something hot or cold.

Upper West Side

As the classic New York neighborhood, the Upper West Side is host to some of New York City's premier cultural institutions. Straddling the border between Harlem and midtown Manhattan, the Upper West Side is one of the most racially diverse neighborhoods in Manhattan. Lincoln Center and Julliard both lend a hand in drawing some of the most talented musicians, dancers, and artists to dot the Upper West Side's colorful streets. Strolling along the wide avenues is comfortable, and nearby Central Park is the perfect place to take a break from shopping.

Verve

❋ 282 Columbus Ave., bet. W. 73rd and 74th Sts.
HOURS: Mon–Sat 11–8; Sun 12–6
PHONE: 212-580-7150

Find a choosy collection of handbags, shoes, and jewelry from all over the world.

Handbags can be a status symbol, but you don't have to shop the designers just because you are in New York. At Verve, owner Steve Ginsberg has established himself as a connoisseur of accessories design. Ginsberg is a lecturer at the Fashion Institute of Technology, and acts as a willing consultant to many young designers who are looking to sell a line of accessories. He's ahead of the curve, and it's nice to see his selections in a less trafficked shopping area.

Verve is a gallery of distinctive, colorful handbags, and no two designs are similar. Find every kind of bag, from beaded clutches, to studded doctor's totes, to leather hobos.

You may recognize some featured designers (Cynthia Rowley, Rafe, Orla Kiely), while others hail from international locales: Italy, Brazil, Spain, and Japan. Bags go anywhere from $40 into the hundreds, depending on size and designer. Unique jewelry ranges from $38–500 also depending on the designer. (Another location: 353 Bleecker Street, bet. W. 10th and Charles Sts., 212-691-6516, Mon–Sat 11–8, Sunday 12–6.)

A cocktail with a view

One of the greatest things about New York City is the vertical expanse of the landscape. Manhattan's skyline, immortalized in film and literature, is breathtaking. Walking around on the street, we very often forget that there is a sea of rooftops, where, perhaps, the city can be appreciated from an even more remarkable vantage point. Fortunately, at these rooftop bars and restaurants, you can enjoy the view of Manhattan, and sip a cocktail while you're at it. These are great places to come rest on your laurels after a hard day of shopping.

At the **Roof Garden Café** at the **Metropolitan Museum of Art** (1000 Fifth Ave. at 82nd St., Fri–Sat 10–8:30, Sun, Tu, Wed, and Thu 10–4:30, closed Mon, 212-535-7710, www.metmuseum.org). If you weren't planning to go for the art (which I'm sure you were) you can enjoy a cocktail overlooking magical Central Park, with that profound skyline peeking up over the trees.

From the narrow terrace that runs along the outside of the rooftop restaurant at the **Beekman Tower** (3 Mitchell Place at 49th St. and 1st Ave., daily 4 p.m.–1 a.m., 212-355-7300), you have a spectacular view of midtown Manhattan. The atmosphere here is a bit on the stuffy side, but if you want to visit a hotel with some old-school flavor—think *The Sweet Smell of Success, The Big Clock*, and other classic Manhattan movies—this is a classic New York joint.

A bit further downtown, overlooking Gramercy Park, is the **High Bar at the Gramercy Park Hotel** (2 Lexington Ave. at 21st St., opens at 4 p.m., 212-475-4320). The beautiful landscaped roof garden, a sanctuary from the street below, first opened in 1926, and the old-world feeling hasn't changed a bit.

Travel a bit west for a hipper, heavier scene at the **Hotel Gansevoort** (18 9th Ave. at W. 13th St., opens at 11 a.m., 212-206-6700) which, in the afternoons, say around 3 or 4 p.m., is a great place to catch a drink while watching the sun start to set over the Hudson. If you go after 6, chances are the bar will be overcrowded with well-heeled after-work drinkers.

Roslyn

�֍ 276 Columbus Ave., at the corner of W. 73rd Street

HOURS: Mon–Sun 11–7

PHONE: 212-496-5050

Trends aside, this eccentric veteran designer knows jewelry like the back of her hand.

Roslyn is a jewelry designer—not professionally affiliated with Steven Alan, her famous downtown-retailing son. However, she's no slouch, having started designing jewelry at age seventeen. She worked with her boyfriend down on the Bowery, near the old Jewelry Exchange, whose recent closing she lamented was "the end of an era." No worries—Roslyn has moved on up, *Jeffersons*-style, to the relaxed environs of the Upper West Side, where her boutique luxuriously wraps around a corner on Columbus Ave. "People here are warm, extremely creative people with great taste. I like to partner with my customers in designing jewelry. They have such great energy," she says.

Roslyn does custom design work. Each piece she makes is infused with her great style and philosophy; if you don't like it, she doesn't hold you to it. She can re-personalize stones (from engagement rings to whatever) to fit a new context and meaning in a person's life. She finds inspiration in European, particularly French, jewelry design, and makes feminine, lacey pieces that can be worn all the time.

The store features over thirty-five hat and jewelry designers, as well as select antique pieces. The jewelry includes diamonds, semi-precious stones, and antique pieces. Jewelry retails for anywhere from $65–500. She also sells vintage watches, which retail for between $300 and $800.

Hat styles run from wide brims to cloches to colorful rain hats by labels like Eugenia Kim, Misa Harada, Kelly Christy, and Jacqueline Lamont. There's a sporty handbag selection as well, by LeSportsac, Cammie Hill, Un Apres Midi de Chien, and Herve Chapelier.

Roslyn's client list includes a lot of mothers and daughters; but she's got stories about everyone from Elizabeth Taylor to Ed Sullivan to Ray Charles back in the day, to the likes of Yoko Ono and Ben Stiller today.

Polish, please

Now that everyone is getting their nails done—women, men, gay, straight—it is a good thing that New York City has the cheapest and best manicures and pedicures, arguably, in the world. Whatever your reason for indulging, whether it's to finish off your look, show off new sandals, or just take a break from shopping, here are some of the best places in the city to get your nails done.

Dashing Diva Nail Spa (multiple locations; visit www.dashingdiva.com). At this cozy nail spot, they serve Cosmos. They are also open early and late, depending on when you have a hole in your busy schedule.

Go Girl (193 E. 4th Street bet. Aves. A and B, 212-473-9973, daily 11–8). Go Girl is a laid-back, super cute, nail salon where you can always find a chair and good conversation with the staff. One day a week, there is a special where you can get both a manicure and pedicure for $25—call the store for details.

Soho Nail (458 W. Broadway, bet. W. Houston and Prince Sts., 3rd floor, 212-475-6368, Mon–Sat 10–8, Sun 12–7). The women at Soho Nail work hard for their money, providing all types of beauty services cheaper and faster than you can say "manicure/pedicure." Most waxing services cost under $30; a manicure/pedicure is around $25. Call ahead for an appointment if you are going during peak hours (after work or on the weekend).

Rescue Beauty Lounge (8 Centre Market Place bet. Broome and Grand Sts., 212-431-0449, Tu–Fri 11–8, Sat–Sun 10–6, www.rescuebeauty.com). This is one of the most popular nail spas in Manhattan, and this location is out of the way and more quiet and relaxing than the others. They will serve you green tea, and scrub and soak your hands and feet with care. They use the popular line of Burt's Bee's products, which are superb, and all-natural lotions and scrubs. Try Rescue's house nail polish brand as well—they make high quality polish in rich colors. My favorite is Film Noir, a profound purple-red that looks stunning on almost any skin tone. In the front of the shop, Rescue also sells accessories and jewelry to go with your shiny new manicure/pedicure. For a full list of services, call one of the stores or consult the website.

Other locations: 21 Cleveland Place, bet. Spring and Kenmare, 212-431-3805, Mon–Fri 11–8, Sat 10–6; 34 Gansevoort Street, bet. Hudson and Greenwich Sts., 212-206-6409, Tu–Fri 11–8, Sat–Sun 10–6).

Angel Feet (77 Perry Street, bet. Bleecker and W. 4th Sts., 212-924-3576, www.angelfeet.com, Mon, Tu, and Fri, 10–9; Wed 1–9; and Sat–Sun 10–8.).

Like its name, Angel Feet promises to take the client straight up to heaven, in less time. The spa offers reflexology treatments in an unhurried, relaxing fashion, taking only two clients at a time. The idea is that this intensive foot massage will relax the whole body, working points that correspond to every major muscle group and organ. Home and office calls can also be arranged.

Upper East Side

New York's Upper East Side bristles with pristine luxury. Some of the city's oldest and wealthiest residents live here—scenes from old movies roll before your eyes as you peek up at the gorgeous building facades and in the windows of ancestral homes. When you're done checking out Museum Mile along Fifth Avenue and taking a walk through Central Park, here are some great little shops to pop into. A bit further west, all along Fifth and Madison avenues are the flagship stores of every major fashion designer.

Sara

✻ 950 Lexington Ave., bet. E. 69th and 70th Sts.
HOURS: Mon–Fri 11–7; Sat 12–6; closed Sun
PHONE: 212-772-3243
WEB: www.saranyc.com

The finest handmade ceramic dinnerware, as well as other decorative items for the home.

The silence is palpable as you step inside this immaculate boutique. Naoki Uemura and his wife have kept shop at this location for fifteen years. He says second and third generations of locals have returned to Sara to behold and buy their exquisite, one-of-a-kind wares. You could spend a good fifteen minutes examining the balance of a tilted bowl, or the perfect thickness of a handmade plate. Uemura buys pieces of art that speak to him. "I hear voices in a small piece of clay, and when they are noisy, I must have them," he says. You can find tea services, single plates, bowls, and cups, as well as vases, urns, and much more, in a variety of ceramic styles and finishes ranging from the very natural to fiery, sparkling glazes. Sleek, modern pieces sit next to organic shapes that beautifully retain the potter's handprint on their surface. Featured artists (they rotate) include Hanako Nakazato, who is a fourteenth-generation potter from Japan, Malcolm Wright, Uko Morita, a Japanese ceramicist working in New York, and many others. Sara also features some blown glass pieces, as well as traditional wall-hanging vases from Japan. "We like high quality with a light price," quips Uemura. You can find a stunning piece for as little as $30 here, perfect for a gift or as an addition to your own collection. Check the website for featured artists, as Uemura and his wife are always traveling and acquiring new works.

Made for you

As Manhattanites go through their daily lives, they have precious few moments when they can express their individuality—play-lists in their iPods as they whisk through subway tunnels, milk with one sugar in morning coffee, desktop settings, and the buttons on their jackets. In Manhattan, cash and the wherewithal will get you to the pinnacle of shopping quickly—customization. In a city that prides itself on the unique experiences it offers, here are ways for you to explore your own style as a means of self-expression.

Custom clothing

Abaete (560 Broadway, Suite 306 bet. Spring and Prince Sts., 212-334-4755, www.abaete.com, open by appointment only for custom and wholesale orders). Abaete is a solid women's collection filled with unusual and delicate details. The feminine dresses are made from silks, cotton toile, twills, and wools. Many of the fabrics have a bit of sheen to them, and gold detail is a signature characteristic of the line. The designs are playful but sophisticated, with details in a knotted neckline, a double-layer shredded skirt, or a graphic print. Swimsuit shapes nod to the designer's Brazilian roots, and the diverse collection includes several sophisticated maillots that recall tan starlets of the '70s. Tops range from $150–400, bottoms $100–300, bathing suits a little pricier at $180. Laura Poretzky, the founder and designer of Abaete, became interested in fashion design as an art student at the Rhode Island School of Design, and has done time in Ralph Lauren's ranks. Abaete is also sold at several multi-label stores, which are also great for finding the staples of each New York fashion season.

Kirna Zabete (96 Greene Street, bet. Prince and Spring Sts., 212-941-9656, www.kirnazabete.com, Mon–Sat 11–7, Sun 12–6) is a well-known destination for fashion.

The more popular **Barney's Co-op** (multiple locations; visit www.barneys.com for addresses and info) caters to a younger customer, and boasts a vast selection of jeans to go with your Abaete top.

Linda Dresner (484 Park Ave. bet. E. 58th and E. 59th Sts., 212-308-3177, www.lindadresner.com, Mon–Sat 10–6), is a multi-label retailer from Chicago on the Upper East Side.

Jussara Lee (11 Little West 12th Street bet. Ninth Ave. and Washington Sts., 212-242-4128, www.jussara-lee.com, daily 11–7, Sun 12–7), custom makes suits, evening dresses, dresses, and more, for the same price you'd pay off the rack. Her Meatpacking boutique has a cold, art gallery feel to it, but if you ask her any questions, you will warm up to her, not to mention her beautiful clothes, quickly. It's simple—choose from bolts and samples of luxury fabrics, one of her fabulous designs, she takes your measurements, and voila! Signature items include minimalist sheer chiffon dresses and skirts, and you're guaranteed to fit her pants (as they are made for you!)

Custom perfumes

Bond No. 9 (9 Bond Street bet. Broadway and Lafayette, 212-228-1732, Mon–Fri 11–8, Sat 11–7, Sun 12–6). What could be more heavenly than a fragrance custom blended per your specifications? Owner Laurice Rahme has stocked her beautiful north of Soho store with a collection of twenty-two scents (and counting) blended to capture the personality of the New York City neighborhoods for which they are named. The most popular ready-to-wear fragrances are Chelsea Flowers and Eau de New York—others are called Little Italy, Madison Soiree, Riverside Drive, So New York, among others. Although she is French, she recently became an American citizen, and decided to give New York some good smells to call their very own.

The fragrance specialists in the store will blend as many fragrances as you like in a 2-oz. custom blend ($45 per fragrance), which you can covet in Bond No. 9's specialty star-shaped perfume bottles ($40–150). They will keep your fragrance recipe on file and charge you about ten dollars less for a refill.

Custom makeup

3 Custom Color Specialists (54 West 22nd Street, 3rd Floor bet. 5th and 6th Aves., www.threecustom.com. To book an appointment, please call 888-262-7714). A visit to this Garment District lab is worth the hunt. Founders Trae Bodge and Chad Hayduk start each session with a quiz. What color are the veins in your wrist? Do you wear silver or gold? Do you burn or tan? The brightly colored products (all from an archive of color dating back to the 1920s) peek through minimal glass displays in this private, intimate studio. Experts blend colors on the premises.

Prices start with a $65 fee for the initial consultation with a color specialist, and $105 if you want to meet one of the founders. (The initial consultation fee can also be applied to any products you end up purchasing.) Then, there's about 90 minutes worth of mixing, fixing, and swirling until every tint is exactly right. Women who are having a hard time finding products to match their skin tone will adore the custom-blended concealers. Best of all, colors are never discontinued, and you can find hard-to-match colors that may have disappeared from the current color lexicon. The studio also offers bridal trials and makeup services. On-site bridal services can be arranged as well, with travel cost and time included in a quoted rate. They offer a free 20-minute consultation for their ready-to-wear makeup.

Kitchen Arts & Letters

❊ 1531 Lexington bet. 93rd and 94th Sts.

HOURS: Mon 1–6; Tu–Fri 10–6:30; Sat 11–6; closed Sun,
and Sat in the summer.

PHONE: 212-876-5550

WEB: www.kitchenartsandletters.com

*Many famous chefs swear this is the best cookbook
store in the country, let alone New York City.*

As food has taken center stage in American magazines and
television, we are becoming accustomed to an international
language for cuisine and cooking. Kitchen Arts & Letters carries nearly 13,000 titles on the subjects of food and wine,
ranging from simple cookery books to scientific and technical
volumes on culinary history, sociology and anthropology, restaurant management, and many other areas, even extending
to food-related fiction. Included are many imported works
in foreign languages—Spanish, German, and more than a
thousand titles in French. At Kitchen Arts & Letters, one can
find cookbooks and books on food from all over the world,
specific to region—for instance, South Indian cooking from
the Indian state of Kerala, or regional Mexican cuisine. The
small, one-room store has shelves floor to ceiling, where
every surface is covered with cookbooks, generally organized
by country and region. The staff is extremely helpful and very
well-versed in food literature.

The owner is Nach Waxman, a former book editor with
deep ties to the food world. The clientele includes a sub-
stantial number of food professionals, and the shop prides
itself on its experienced staff, many of whom have worked
in the food industry as bartenders, chefs, and restauranteurs.
Whether you are looking for Edward Dabner's charming
book on the food of the Appalachian region, or the excellent
Gambero Rosso volume on Italian wines, or Colette Rossant's

book on the lost food of Egypt, this is the place to go. The store also deals extensively in out-of-print food books, offering a free search service to meet customer needs, and will ship books anywhere in the world. Mr. Waxman will personally send you an annotated new arrivals list three times a year by e-mail, if you request it.

Kitchen-happy

For a passionate cook, nothing's more fun than an obscure kitchen utensil. Because New York's restaurant community is so large and diverse, shoppers have access to the stores that the chefs shop in. This is a short list of stores to visit if you are in the market for that special something for the kitchen.

The J.B. Prince Company (36 East 31st Street, 11th Floor, bet. Park and Madison Aves., 212-683-3553, open Mon–Fri 9–5, www.jbprince.com).

J.B. Prince is a gallery stocked with everything from basic peppermills and strainers, to more esoteric items, including quail egg cutters and a mechanism that cuts cucumbers and potatoes into cups, as well as tools never seen outside of professional kitchen, like sausage-making machines and baker's scales. The showroom is located on the 11th floor of a random office building, and can make a gadget addict out of any home cook. One of the best things about the store is the selection of knives. They stock the Henkles, Wüstoff, and Global lines—from Japan, they carry Misono knives (a company with a 750-year history and a descendant of one of Japan's greatest sword makers!), as well as Japanese Professional, MAC, Masahiro, and Bunmei. All of these knives are incredibly thin and sharp for fine slicing. The store also carries cleavers, saws, and various other tools for butchering. From the near-secret location, to the business cards of every great restaurant/caterer in the city and country posted on the bulletin boards flanking the doorway (all faithful customers, mind you), shopping at J.B. Prince makes you feel like a restaurant professional, or at least like you are pretty tight with one.

Broadway Panhandler (65 E. 8th St. bet. Broadway and University, 212-966-3434, www.broadwaypanhandler.com, Mon–Sat 11–7, Sun 11–6). This store sells everything for the home chef; it's a true one-stop shop. They have a wonderful selection of brands, like AllClad, Le Creuset, and Krups, as well as all the coolest accessories you never knew you needed—until now.

Korin (57 Warren Street bet. W. Broadway and Church Sts., 800-626-2172, Mon–Sat 10–6, www.korin.com), specializes in Asian eating accoutrement. If you've ever wanted to take home the sake set, the chopsticks, the plates, the bowls, or the bamboo steamers from a Japanese restaurant, a trip to Korin is essential. Korin is a restaurant supplier to hotels and restaurants worldwide, but you can also buy their beautiful porcelain tableware, and more, for your own home.

Bridge Kitchenware (711 3rd Ave., enter on 45th St. 212-688-4220, Mon–Fri 9–6, Sat 10–4, www.bridgekitchenware.com) sells every kind of bakeware, cookware, and knife imaginable. Need that six-inch fry pan, or that saucepan that cooks the perfect amount of pasta for two? Look no further.

Bowery Kitchen Supply, (460 West 16th St. at the corner of Ninth Ave., 212-376-4982, open Mon–Sat 10–7, Sun 11–6, www.bowerykitchens.com). This commercial restaurant supplier brings a piece of the Bowery's kitchen supply district into the Chelsea Market, where tenants are handpicked for their connection to food. Open for over ten years, the owners specialize in commercial-grade high-quality cookware, which despite looking old-fashioned and unwieldy at times, is just as good (and a heck of a lot cheaper) than the cookware you will find at Williams Sonoma. Bowery Kitchen Supply also sells all kinds of gadgets for prepping food, including ones like your grandmother used. They sell cutlery by the piece. Most customers who shop here know what they want. If you've seen a chef on TV using a gadget, or read about one recently, chances are you will find it here.

Tribeca

The land of New York City's wealthiest and most tasteful citizens, Tribeca has become a destination for visitors and locals alike. The Tribeca Film Festival, Robert DeNiro, and other New York City institutions all call the neighborhood home. Tribeca is full of old printing houses and today, many film production companies. The Soho and Tribeca Grand Hotels both boast beautiful bars and great music—and Battery Park is just a short bike ride away.

Number (N)ine

✳ 431 Washington Street, bet. Vestry and Desbrosses Sts.
HOURS: Mon–Sat 11–7; closed Tu; Sun 12–6
PHONE: 212-431-8699
WEB: www.numberniners.com

Designer Takahiro Miyashita sells one of Japan's top men's brands in this hidden Tribeca boutique.

Number (N)ine is a lovely, haunting space: dark wood with intricately chosen hangings and lamps lingering in corners of the store—it could have been the room behind the swinging bookcase in an Ingmar Bergman film. The main chandelier is lifted from an old Morton Street townhouse, fittingly oxidized by cigarette smoke. The two imposing metal doors in the back of the space were imported from Hungary, and the ceiling is covered in seventeen different patterned tin tiles from around the world. The clothing racks are made from gateposts, culminating in the designer's vision for the retail equivalent of Transylvania.

Miyashita utilizes old-world tailoring and luxe fabrics to create clothing that feels accessible, but is totally unique.

Pieces are not produced in bulk to prevent counterfeiting in Japan, where the store frequently sells out of each item in a matter of hours. The designer maintains a strong point of view, and each piece in the collection is part of a theme. He riffs on the androgyny of horror films and the gothic subculture, as well as the ever-changing boundary between street and formal wear. There are strong musical influences, such as punk and rockabilly, in every collection. Leathers have been washed and wrinkled, and some pieces utilize wire to stand stiff. The Number (N)ine customer is *definitely* not afraid to take risks. Shoe styles include unusual variations on sneakers, and lace-up boots with curled and pointed toes. Sleeveless jackets, long hooded sweatshirts, and kilts round out the imaginative collection. Accessories include black-on-black studded belts, bracelets, and cuffs. The store also carries its own line of womenswear called 9, designed by Miyashita's assistant, as well as a men's and women's denim line called N(N) by Number (N)ine.

Most of the looks in this store are perfect for the young, savvy, stylish man with some money to burn—most pieces are expensive to very expensive (from $300 to $10,000). A great place to buy a gift for a fashion-forward friend or relative.

Button-up, button-down

While New York hasn't quite caught up to the Savile Row standard of London, there are some good places to find a shirt for a man for any occasion. A sartorially keen buddy of mine gravely told me, "Unfortunately, the dearth of good spots for shirts means that these are also on the pricier side." The upside is when he dons a shirt or tie or suit from any of these places, he always turns heads. Oh, and each of these boutiques also carries women's shirts—but his are the reason to go!

Paul Smith (108 Fifth Ave. at 16th Street, 212-627-9770, Mon–Sat 11–7, Thu 11–8, Sun 12–6, www.paulsmith.co.uk). This classic British menswear designer is touted for his bold approach to fabric, pattern, and color, that stick to traditional old-world styling. Smith has also gone on to design accessories, housewares, and furniture. Prices for shirts start at $150.

At **Thomas Pink** (10 Columbus Circle at W. 58th St., 212-823-9650; 1155 Ave. of the Americas, 212-840-9663; 520 Madison Ave., 212-838-1928, www.thomaspink.com), the shirts sit prettily inside their many suits of checkers, herringbones, stripes, and solids. It's a veritable forest of beautiful shirts, and the name says it all—British, cheeky, and slick. Shirts average $140, from casual to dress shirts.

Seize Sur Vingt (243 Elizabeth Street bet. E. Houston and Prince Sts., 212-343-0476, Mon–Sat 11–7, Sun 12–6, www.16sur20.com). At this cool Nolita boutique, find two simple racks of near-perfect shirts along either wall that will undoubtedly make him feel like an international man of mystery. Fabrics are the specialty here, finely woven and in beautiful hues. Shirts are $140 to $160; pants from $250 to $300; and suits from $1,175 to $1,250.

Ina (262 Mott Street bet. E. Houston and Prince Sts., 212-334-2210, daily 12–7, www.inanyc.com), is a consignment store specializing in men's fashion (there is a women's store right around the corner at 21 Prince Street). Wares are in mint condition, and prices are reasonably slashed.

Odin (328 E. 11th Street bet. First and Second Aves., 212-475-0666, Mon–Sat 12–9, Sun 12–8, www.odinnewyork.com). Odin's owners fluidly combine the best of streetwear and tailored clothing for men, with a home and lifestyle element, including shaving, hair, and bath products (from Sharp's and Korress, among others), bags, art and photography books, pillows, skateboards, unisex jewelry, and much more. This small East Village store has been a quiet trendsetter, and could be what men in the city have been waiting for. Shirts cost around $135; pants around $175; and blazers and jackets start at $275. (Also located at: 199 Lafayette St. bet. Spring and Broome Sts., 212-966-0026, Mon–Sat 11–8, Sun 11–7.)

South Brooklyn
(Prospect Heights/Clinton Hill)

South Brooklyn has a slightly different vibe from Williamsburg—it is more residential and tree-lined. As such, shopping in this part of Brooklyn can be very relaxing, and the shops are set up to cater to a wandering customer, turning up on a random corner or in the middle of a block of houses. If you are a Manhattanite thinking about moving to the calm environs of Brooklyn, maybe a little shopping trip is what you need to start exploring this most excellent borough. Businesses are popping up—a raw food restaurant, a shop called Bicycle Station (560 Vanderbilt Ave., bet Bergen and Dean Sts.), and an outpost of the popular Manhattan café Le Gamin (556 Vanderbilt Ave., bet. Bergen and Dean Sts.), to name a few.

Re-Pop

�֍ 68 Washington Avenue bet. Willoughby and
Myrtle Aves.
HOURS: Tu–Fri 11–7; Sat 11–8:30; Sun 11–6
PHONE: 718-260-8032
WEB: www.repopny.com

A vintage gallery that combines the overcrowded charm of an old-fashioned Parisian boutique with the promising clutter of a midwestern junk shop.

Re-Pop lies on the northern edge of Fort Greene and Clinton Hill, just south of the Brooklyn Navy Yard. Many artists have moved from overcrowded Williamsburg to this area. Re-Pop fits right in, reflecting an artists' sensibility in their furnishings and decorating offerings. Anyone who's shopped for vintage and antiques in the city knows that the prices can be a doozy, which is why owners Carl Grauer and Russell Boyle—both artists themselves—provide "the most innovative and unique of historical pieces at equitable prices." You can find everything from doll heads, American folk art, antique chemical bottles, and taxidermy, to more modern items including furniture, lighting, and much more. You're also likely to see the names of noted designers such as Kent Coffey, Paul McCobb, Eero Saarinen, Adrian Pearsall for Craft Associates, and Milo Baughman, though "since we are a resale shop, we go with what we can find from week to week. But usually a few of these designers are represented here," says Russell. If you're not originally from New York City, or just visiting, you'll find Re-Pop's vibe similar to your favorite hometown thrift store: a place you'll want to visit again and again to score the conversation pieces you'll brag about.

Pieces of Brooklyn

�֎ 671 Vanderbilt Ave., at Park Place

HOURS: Mon by appt. only; Tu–Thu 11–7; Fri & Sat 11–8; Sun 11–6

PHONE: 718-857-7211

WEB: www.piecesofbklyn.com

228 W. 135th Street

HOURS: Tu–Thu 12–8; Fri & Sat 11–9; Sun 12–6; closed Mon

PHONE: 212-234-7425

WEB: www.piecesofharlem.com

A multi-label men's and women's clothing store specializing in fashion-forward local labels that you won't find in a department store.

Owners Latisha and Colin Daring are a husband-wife styling and retail powerhouse who brought great fashion to this side of Brooklyn. Pieces is located on an out-of-the-way street you may pass on your way to or from lovely Prospect Park. The designers at Pieces embody the hip Bohemian vibe of the neighborhood. Most pieces are casual streetwear or wear-to-work items that have been reworked and detailed with sassy, fun touches. Find, for instance, a pair of beautifully tailored trousers with a brightly colored ribbon sewn down the leg seam, or a high-necked blouse with a ruffled edge in neon green. The pieces stylize fashion trends to reflect the aesthetic of real street fashion, rather than trends dictated by the runways. It's worth a trip just to check out how street style answers the bland cloned mannequins in department stores. Designers include R. Scott French, Sherri Bodell, Joe's Jeans, Anne Ferriday, True Couture, Private Circle, Anja Flint, Catch a Fire, Fillippa, By Caesar, Petra Barazza, Robert Graham, and Year Of. Clothes range from $30–500, depending on the item; average price for shoes is $150.

Knitting

Knit New York (307 E. 14th Street at Second Avenue, 212-387-0707, hours www.knitnewyork.com). This cool cafe is a soothing destination for tired urbanites seeking peace of mind. You'll find both the Brooklyn designer, and his mom, hanging out here. Sign up for a full selection of coffee/espresso and tea beverages, as well as fine baked goods. The store sells skeins of beautiful yarns and knitting supplies. They also offer colorfully named knitting classes as well, like "Sox and Lox" (a brunch time class on Sundays) and Ten Man Mons (for men who want to learn this feminine craft in the company of other dudes). See the website for details.

A bit further south, in Soho, is **Purl** (137 Sullivan Street bet. W. Houston and Prince Sts., 212-420-8796, www.purlsoho.com, Mon–Fri 12–7, Sat and Sun 12–6) a tiny yarn and knitting shop that offers colorful varieties of beautiful yarns from all over the world. The owners have done a lot with a little bit of space—the square table in the middle of the shop makes it easy to peruse, and the walls are lined with hundreds of cubbies filled with yarn. There are also racks of magazines and books from all over the world to browse for more information on what's happening in the world of knitting—a pastime experiencing a big resurgence among New Yorkers. This is a great place to pick up the habit, or to buy a gift for a special someone who loves to knit. Prices can be found on the website, where the full catalog of the store is available for shipping, with photos of yarn detail.

Finding fabrics

Treasure hunting in the Garment District in Manhattan can be fun, if you have some time to poke around. If you are looking for something special to spruce up your tiny studio apartment, like a new pillow cover or something more ambitious, like new curtains, a visit to W. 38th and W. 39th Streets between 6th and 7th Avenues is in order. Located right around the corner from the Parsons School of Design, you may see many fashion students poking around the bolts of fabric. As there are dozens of little fabric shops to visit it can be intimidating, but here is an introduction to a few of the best shops in the area, recommended by designers and stylists.

At **Fabrics Garden** (250 W. 39th Street, bet. 7th and 8th Aves., 212-354-6193, open Mon–Fri 9:30–7:30, Sat 10–7, Sun 12–5, www.fabricsgardenny.com), the vendors specialize in stretch fabrics, bridal fabrics, and reproductions of designer fabric (for instance, if there is a Prada skirt that is tie-dyed, they will have a version of the same fabric here). You should never pay too much, as the prices are always negotiable. An average price for fabric here is $5 per yard. Make sure you examine the bolts of fabric before you buy, as some have been sitting around the shop or in the sun, and may have faded with time. Another great store along these lines is **Neon Fabrics** (239 W. 39th Street, bet. 7th and 8th Aves., 212-221-9705, open Mon–Fri 9–7, and Sat–Sun 10–6), which specializes in brightly colored, and neon-colored fabrics.

A trip to **Leather Impact** (256 W. 38th Street, bet. 7th and 8th Aves., 212-302-2332, open Mon–Fri 9:30–5, www.leatherimpact.com) is like a trip into a colorful tannery. The shop smells of fresh leather, and hundreds of felts line the tables and walls in different colors. If you are trying to color-match something, the salespeople will present you with at least three different options; an average skin costs $30 (depending on the size). They also sell rope and trimming, which is especially good for repairing a broken strap on a handbag, or for leather shoelaces. Leather Impact also stocks embellished leathers, like laser-cut leather, as well as branded and designed leather. This is one of the coolest stores to visit in the Garment District.

index of the new york book of shops (a to z)

index by shop type

Acknowledgments

I'd like to thank my family, as well as the publisher and the editorial team at Rizzoli, for making a second edition of this book possible.

Thank you, also, to all the stores for your time and participation in making this book a success.

About the Author

Ranjani Gopalarathinam is a writer living in New York City. In addition to working on the staff of *Glamour* magazine, her work on fashion, music, and art has appeared in magazines like *Fader*, *Time Out New York*, *Soma*, and *metro.pop*. This is her first book.